Brilliant Bags

Brilliant Bags

20 Beautiful Bags to Stitch and Love

Deena Beverley

MITCHELL BEAZLEY

For Daisy: a brilliant co-designer, fabulous friend,
and all-round superstar daughter.

Brilliant Bags
by Deena Beverley

First published in Great Britain in 2006 by Mitchell Beazley,
an imprint of Octopus Publishing Group Ltd,
2–4 Heron Quays, London E14 4JP

ISBN-13: 978 1 84533 178 8
ISBN-10: 1 84533 178 8

A CIP record for this book is available from the British Library

Set in Bembo and DIN

Colour reproduction by Chroma Graphics, Singapore
Printed and bound in China by Toppan Printing Company Ltd

Senior Executive Editor Anna Sanderson
Executive Art Editors Christine Keilty, Auberon Hedgecoe
Senior Editor Emily Anderson
Editor Karen Hemingway
Design DW Design
Production Seyhan Esen, Faizah Malik

Contents

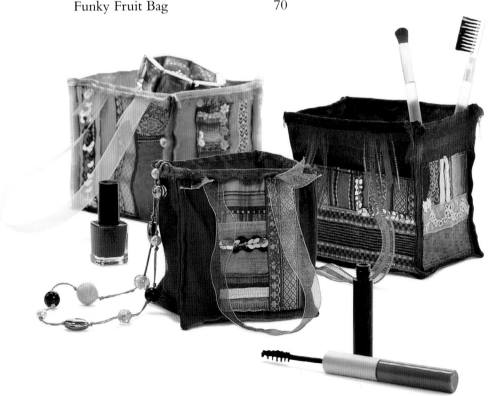

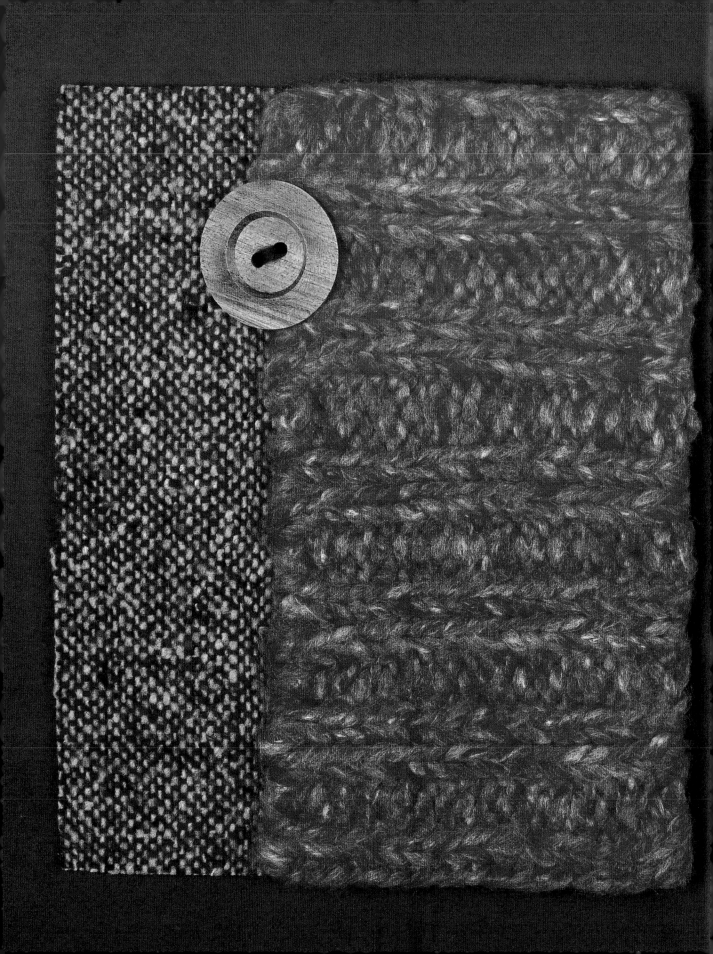

Polo Neck Sweater Bag

With its woollen "neckline" and textured tweed, this soft squashy bag is equally at home in town or country. Choose buttons to accentuate the feel you want to create.

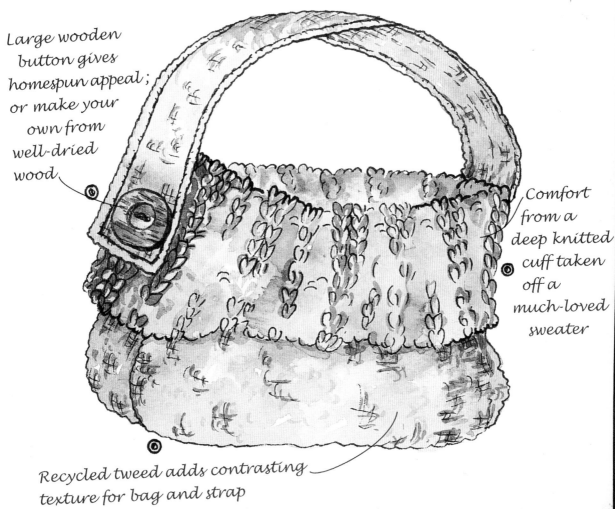

Large wooden button gives homespun appeal; or make your own from well-dried wood

Comfort from a deep knitted cuff taken off a much-loved sweater

Recycled tweed adds contrasting texture for bag and strap

Polo Neck Sweater Bag

On the Paris Métro I spotted a terrifyingly chic lady sporting a knife-sharp suit accessorized with a slouchy sort of handbag, which clearly had a designer price tag as scary as her immaculately maquillaged glare. The soft contours of the tweedy bag were topped with a generously deep cuff of ribbed cashmere knit. My frugal creative streak went into overdrive as I mentally started cutting up thrift-shop jumpers and coats to make an equally delicious version at a fraction of the price.

MATERIALS/CUTTING LIST

Face fabric tweed or own choice
front and back: 2 pieces 37x27cm
(14¾x10½in)
sides and base: 14x83cm (5½ x33in)
strap: 60x15cm (24 x6in)

Firm iron-on interfacing
front and back: 2 pieces 37x27cm
(14¾x10½in)
sides and base: 14x83cm (5½ x33in)
strap: 60x15cm (24 x6in)

Sewing thread to match the face fabric

Lining fabric woolly jumper
front and back: 2 pieces
42.5x55.5cm (17x22in)

Scrap of wool yarn to attach the buttons

2 large wooden buttons

Tapestry needle

SEE PAGE 121 FOR TEMPLATES
Enlarge the templates to the percentages given, using a photocopier if necessary.

MAKING THE OUTSIDE OF THE BAG

Iron the interfacing onto the reverse of all the face fabrics. Transfer the template outline to the fabric and cut out. Pin, baste, and stitch the sides and base piece to the front piece, right sides facing and stitching up to the seam allowance. Attach the back piece in the same way to complete the main bag **(A)**. Clip into the seam allowance around the curved corners, press the seams open, and turn the bag right side out.

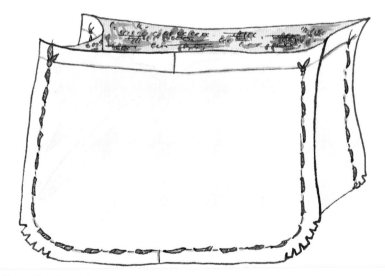

A Baste the three pieces of the bag together.

A single broad strap adds chic gravitas.

A carefully chosen button enhances the countrified look.

This little strap with its buckle, salvaged from a broken bag, makes a great keyring.

As an alternative to tweed you could use another suitably bucolic texture, such as jumbo corduroy or a patchwork of tweed and corduroy.

The squashy shape retains just enough structure to give a modern look, equally at home in town or country.

Leabharlanna Fhine Gall

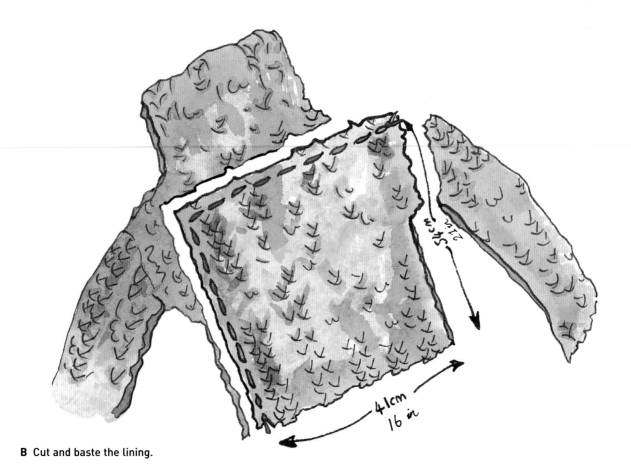

B Cut and baste the lining.

41cm
16 in

53cm
21in

MAKING THE JUMPER LINING

Turn the jumper inside out. Cut off the arms
and neck. Cut the two pieces, measuring from the
bottom edge of the jumper. Align the two pieces.
Pin, baste, and stitch three edges together, leaving
the bottom edge and part of one side open **(B)**.

ATTACHING THE JUMPER LINING

Place the bag inside the jumper, right sides facing,
aligning the hem of the jumper and the raw top
edge of the bag, and each side seam of the lining
with the centre line of the bag sides. Pin, baste, and
stitch the lining to the bag around the top edge **(C)**.

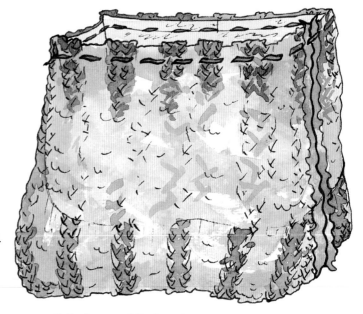

C Baste around the top edge
to attach the lining to the bag.

FINISHING THE BAG

Turn the lining right side out through the opening. Slipstitch the opening closed **(D)**. Arrange the lining so it fills the bottom of the bag and spills over the top edge of the bag to form a deep cuff.

MAKING THE STRAP

Fold the strap fabric in half lengthwise, right sides facing. Pin, baste, and stitch along the long open edge. Press the seam open and turn the right side out. Place the seam centrally, turn in the raw ends by 1.5cm (⅝in). Topstitch all around the strap, close to the edge **(E)**.

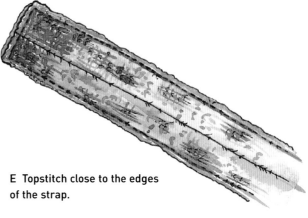

E Topstitch close to the edges of the strap.

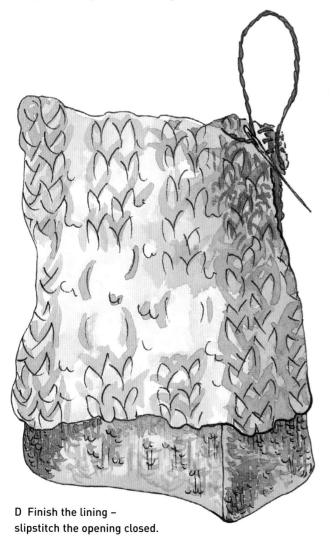

D Finish the lining – slipstitch the opening closed.

ATTACHING THE STRAP

Pin, baste, and stitch the strap to the bag 2.5cm (1in) from the upper edge in the centre of each side panel. Attach a button at each end of the strap using a tapestry needle threaded with wool **(F)**.

F Attach the buttons using a tapestry needle and wool.

Naïve Portrait Bag

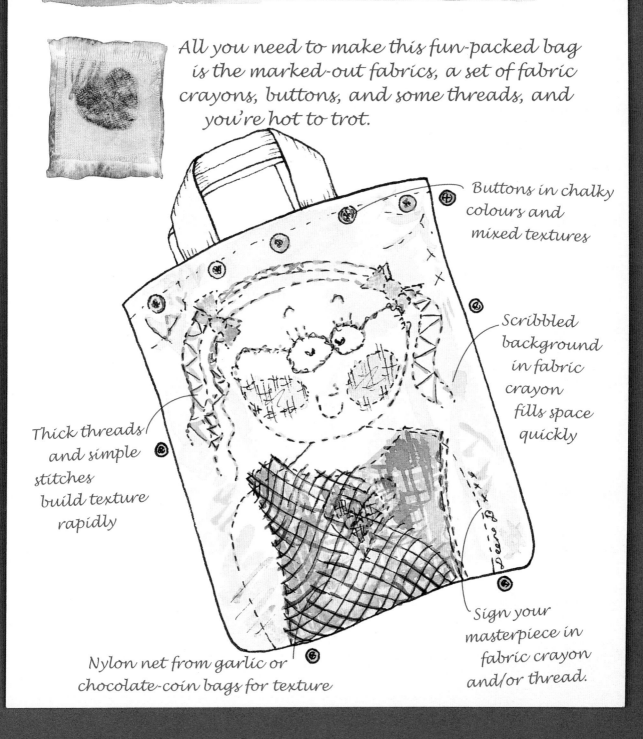

All you need to make this fun-packed bag is the marked-out fabrics, a set of fabric crayons, buttons, and some threads, and you're hot to trot.

Buttons in chalky colours and mixed textures

Scribbled background in fabric crayon fills space quickly

Thick threads and simple stitches build texture rapidly

Sign your masterpiece in fabric crayon and/or thread.

Nylon net from garlic or chocolate-coin bags for texture

Naïve Portrait Bag

Anyone lucky enough to have a child in their life is inevitably the recipient of many a lovingly produced work of art. When the fridge has almost collapsed beneath the weight of their offerings, it's time to immortalize one of their creations on this adorable little bag, perfectly sized to hold a sketch book and pencils.

MATERIALS/CUTTING LIST

Thick black marker pen and paper
or a photocopy of an existing drawing
Non-marking sticky tape
Water-soluble fabric marker pen
Selection of fabric crayons
Selection of embroidery cottons
stranded cotton and cotton perlé
to tone with crayon colours
Scraps of organza and nylon net
Selection of buttons
25cm (10in) embroidery hoop
Embroidery needle
Sturdy calico
front and reverse: 2 pieces 35x35cm
(14x14in), trimmed after embellishment
to 24x27cm (9½x10½in)
handles: 2 pieces 9x32cm (3½x12½in)
Lining fabric to tone with drawing
2 pieces 24x27cm (9½x10½in)
Sewing thread to match fabric

CREATING THE NAÏVE PORTRAIT

If you don't have an existing drawing, sketch a simple self-portrait in thick black marker pen on paper. Or if an existing drawing is too complex, photocopy it and pick out the main outlines on the copy in thick black marker pen. Tape the drawing to a flat surface.

TRANSFERRING THE DRAWING

Tape a piece of calico over the drawing. Using the removable fabric marker pen, mark out the seam allowance and cutting lines. Sketch the outline of the drawing onto the calico and colour it with fabric crayons **(A)**. Colour scraps of fabric and net with crayons for appliqué use. Fix the colours, using the manufacturer's directions.

EMBROIDERING THE DESIGN

Place the calico in the embroidery hoop. Work running stitch and stem stitch around the outlines of the design. Weave thread between the rows of stitches to create hair. Stitch on appliqué and buttons, as desired **(B)**.

MAKING UP THE BAG

Follow the instructions for a basic lined tote bag (*see* p.118).

A Colour the design on calico using a fabric crayon.

B Add the details with stitch and appliqué.

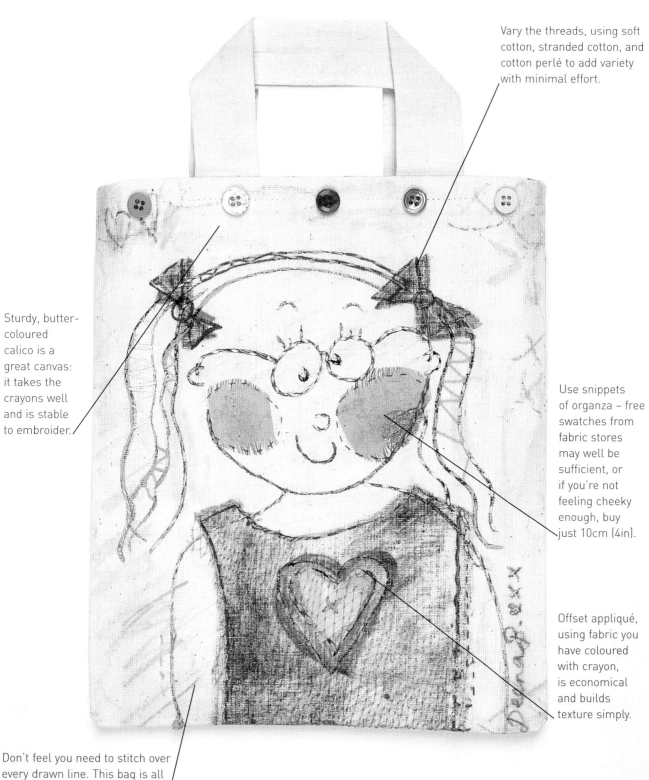

Vary the threads, using soft cotton, stranded cotton, and cotton perlé to add variety with minimal effort.

Sturdy, butter-coloured calico is a great canvas: it takes the crayons well and is stable to embroider.

Use snippets of organza – free swatches from fabric stores may well be sufficient, or if you're not feeling cheeky enough, buy just 10cm (4in).

Offset appliqué, using fabric you have coloured with crayon, is economical and builds texture simply.

Don't feel you need to stitch over every drawn line. This bag is all about fun, so make it as densely or sparsely stitched as you like.

Mary Poppins Overnighter

Be like a supermodel and always fly with overnight essentials in your hand luggage, in case of baggage-handling disasters. This overnighter keeps all your must-haves safe.

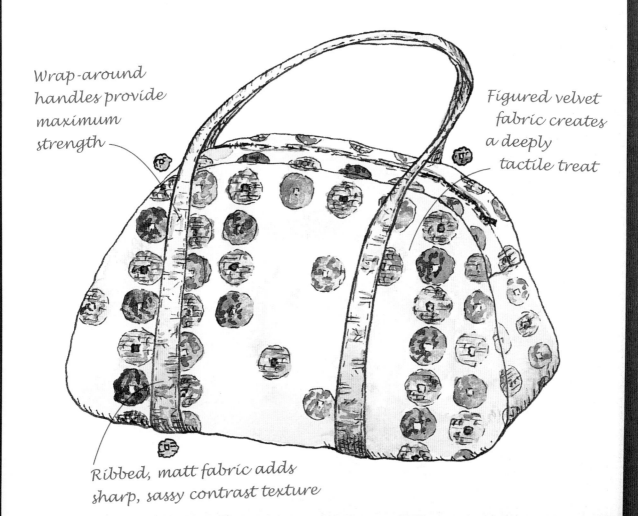

Wrap-around handles provide maximum strength

Figured velvet fabric creates a deeply tactile treat

Ribbed, matt fabric adds sharp, sassy contrast texture

Mary Poppins Overnighter

I've never understood the appeal of the ubiqutous brown and tan monogrammed luggage favoured by celebs. To me it looks plasticky, cold, and even (hands over ears all compulsive über-spenders) more than a tad cheap. This luscious, squashy alternative uses a deep-pile furnishing fabric for "sink-in-and-never-want-to-climb-out-again" country-house sofa appeal. Using an unusual upholstery fabric also means you need never again risk drowning in confusion as a sea of identical luggage swirls about you in airport baggage reclaim.

MATERIALS/CUTTING LIST

Face fabric
front and back: 2 pieces 48x28cm (19x11in)
sides and base: 17x90cm (6¾x35½in)
zip panels: 2 pieces 9.5x50cm (3¾x20in)
handles: 233x6cm (93x2¼in)
zip ends: 2 folded fabric scraps
approx. 6x6cm (2¼x2¼in)
Lining
front and back: 2 pieces 48x28cm (19x11in)
sides and base: 17x90cm (6¾x35½in)
zip panels: 2 pieces 8.5x50cm (3¾x20in)
Firm iron-on interfacing
sufficient to back all face and lining fabric
Zip 35cm (14in) long
Sewing thread to match fabrics
Soft plastic tubing 2 lengths
50cm (20in) x 6mm (⅜in) diam.
SEE PAGE 122 FOR TEMPLATE
Enlarge the template by 300%,
using a photocopier if necessary.

CUTTING OUT THE BAG

Iron the interfacing onto the wrong side of all the face fabric and lining pieces. Transfer the markings from the template onto the wrong side of the interfaced face fabric and lining pieces. Cut out the pieces.

MAKING THE ZIPPED PANEL

Fold each piece of zip end fabric in half widthways. Baste the zip ends onto the right side of the zip tape, 30cm (12in) apart and folded edges toward the zip **(A)**.

A Baste the zip ends to the zip tape.

Press under the seam allowance along the zip edge of the zip panel pieces. Pin and baste these, placed centrally, onto the right side of the zip tape **(B)**.

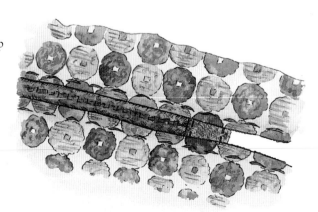

B Baste the zip panels to the zip.

The handles are filled with soft plastic tubing for added strength and comfort when carrying.

The sleek contemporary fabric brings fresh modernity to a nostalgic shape.

ATTACHING THE ZIP PANEL LINING

Pin and baste the right side of each zip panel lining to the zip tape, aligning one long raw edge of the lining with each edge of the tape on the wrong side of the assembled zip panel (C). Press the lining to align with the face fabric.

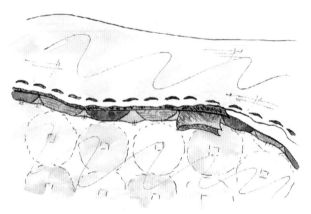

C Baste the lining to the zip tape.

SECURING THE ZIP

Pin, baste, and topstitch through all the layers close to the zip. Begin and end the stitch line 1cm (⅜in) beyond the opening, securing the zip ends. Pin, baste, and stitch the remaining open seam of the face fabric at each end of the zip, right sides facing. Stop 1.5cm (½in) from the topstitching, taking care not to catch the lining or zip ends. Slipstitch the face fabric to the zip ends (D).

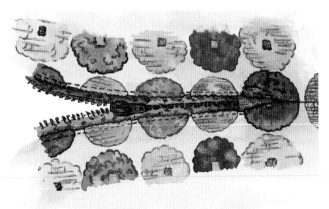

D Close the seam but leave
a gap for the zip end.

Pin, baste, and stitch the remaining open seam of lining. Slipstitch in place as before, taking care the stitches do not show on the right side. Press and then leave the zip open.

ASSEMBLING THE BAG LINING

Pin and baste the lining sides and base piece to each end of the zip panel, right sides facing and taking care not to catch the face fabric. Pin the front piece to the new zip panel, matching the markings. Adjust and trim the length of the sides panels if necessary. Remove the front piece. Stitch the zip panel seams and press them open. Pin, baste, and stitch the lining front and back pieces to the new zip panel, matching the markings and leaving a 15cm (6in) opening along one bottom seam for turning. Press the seams open and clip into the seam allowance around the curves (E).

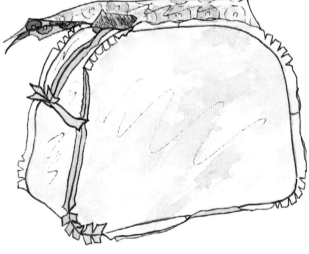

E Clip into the seam allowance
of the curves on the lining.

ASSEMBLING THE FACE FABRIC

Pin, baste, and stitch the face front and back panels centrally to the long panel, right sides facing, stitching along the lower straight edge of these panels only, not around the curves. Press the seams open.

MAKING AND ATTACHING THE HANDLES

Press the seam allowance towards the wrong side along both long edges of the handle fabric. Turn one short end under and baste, then stitch it over the other end. Pin, baste, and stitch it in place 7.5cm (3in) on either side of the centre line across the base, front, and back panels (F).

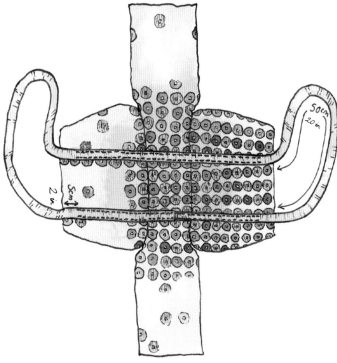

F Stitch the handle fabric in place along the base, front, and back panels.

Finish off the stitching at each end of each handle with a square of reinforcing stitches 5cm (2in) in from the top raw edges of the front and back panels.

FINISHING THE HANDLES

Position one length of plastic tubing centrally on the wrong side of each handle loop. Pin, baste, and topstitch in place (G).

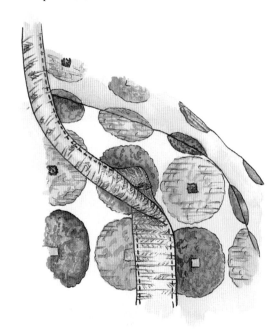

G Topstitch the handles over the tubing.

ASSEMBLING THE BAG

Pin, baste, and stitch together the face fabric pieces to assemble them in the same way as the lining, but without leaving an opening for turning. Turn the bag right side out through the lining and slipstitch the opening closed. Secure the lining to the face fabric through the seam allowance with a few small hand stitches.

Circular Felt Bag

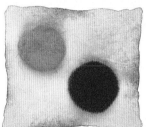

Bags don't get much jollier than this. Sophisticated colours give this childlike design a grown-up edge, making it suitable for mother and daughter to share, or rather fight over!

Layer different felts for lively contrast

Blanket stitch around the edge is quick to work

A "glove-ly" detachable doll makes this a great gift

Circular Felt Bag

OK, I admit it – I got carried away here. Many of my designs feature detachable corsages, as their double usefulness really appeals to my frugal nature. However, this felt bag not only has a doll in addition to the corsage, but the doll (Ditsy by name) even has her own handbag. At my daughter's suggestion, I toyed briefly with the idea of the doll having a doll, with a handbag that opened to reveal a doll who had a doll who had a handbag, etc, but perhaps that's a project for another day!

MATERIALS/CUTTING LIST
Curved and beading needles
Pinking shears
Scraps of new or recycled fabric, felt, ribbon
Cotton perlé, soft, and stranded cottons
Assorted small buttons and 1 tiny bead
Sewing thread to match fabrics
BAG
Thick wool felt
main bag: 2 pieces 33x33cm (13x13in)
pocket: 11x17cm (4¼x6¾in)
contrast strip: 3.5x30cm (1⅜x12in)
Marbled felt: 17.5x25cm (7x9¾in)
Lining fabric: 2 pieces 25x33cm (10x13in)
Firm iron-on interfacing: 2 pieces
25x33cm (10x13in)
CORSAGE
Brooch finding
Thick wool felt
circle, 6cm (2¼in) diam.
circle, 3.5cm (1⅜in) diam. with pinked edge
3 leaf shapes 3.5x5cm (1⅜x2in), one with
pinked edge
3 rectangles 1.5x4cm (½x1½in)
DOLL
Child's stripy glove
Scraps of fleecy felt
Thick PVA craft adhesive
Chenille stem
Old sock in beige or flesh colour
Assorted bouclé yarn for hair
Spun-paper ball 2cm (¾in) diam.
SEE PAGE 122 FOR TEMPLATE
Enlarge template to 280%,
using a photocopier if necessary.

MAKING THE PETALS
Take the larger circle of felt and secure a length of contrasting cotton perlé on the wrong side. Stitch up through the centre of the felt, take the thread around the edge of the circle, and bring the needle up through the centre again. Pull the thread slightly to start to form petal shapes. Repeat twice more to make three petals. Secure the thread on the wrong side **(A)**.

A Wrap the cotton perlé around the felt to make petals.

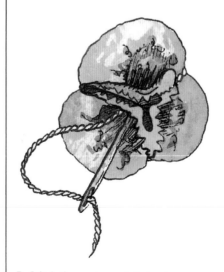

B Stitch the centre petals in place.

FINISHING THE CORSAGE
Place the smaller circle of felt on top of the flower and secure it with a small stitch through its centre. With your fingers, push the underside of the felt into the centre and secure it with a small stitch. Repeat twice to form three petals **(B)**. Add simple decorative stitches to the felt leaf shapes. Stitch together the leaves, the small rectangles of felt, and the flower onto the brooch finding.

Quick, big stitches
are simple and
fun to work
in soft cotton
thread.

Thick wool felt
is a luxurious yet
informal fabric,
which suits the
bag's youthful and
exuberant styling.

Soothingly smooth, matt buttons
in different shapes are worth
seeking out for their contrasting texture.

Mix it up! Floral ribbon
from a special party
hairstyle tops a fragment
of cherished corduroy
trousers. Kids will love
having their favourite
clothes immortalized
with such panache.

MAKING THE BAG AND POCKET

Cut out the felt for the bag, contrast strip, and marbled panel using the templates. Position the marbled felt on the bag. Using running stitch in embroidery thread, add the contrast strip. Stitch on ribbons and buttons and fold over the top of the pocket towards the front. Stitch the pocket to the bag **(C)**.

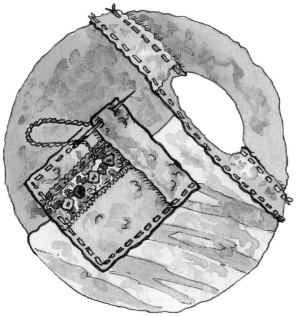

C Decorate the bag front with the contrast strip and attach the pocket.

ASSEMBLING THE BAG

With right sides facing, pin, baste, and stitch the front and back of the bag together around the outer edge **(D)**. Turn the bag right side out and glue on the panel of marbled felt.

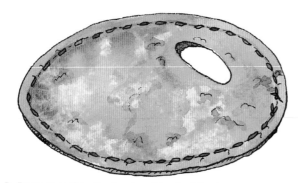

D Baste together the front and back of the bag.

MAKING THE LINING

Iron interfacing onto the wrong side of the lining fabric. Cut out the lining using the template. Pin, baste, and stitch the lining pieces together, right sides facing, around the curved edge **(E)**. Clip into the seam allowance around the curve and turn the lining right side out. Press the straight seam allowances towards the wrong side.

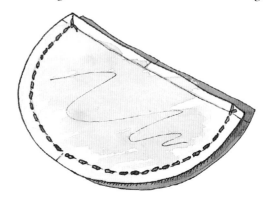

E Baste the lining pieces together.

FINISHING THE BAG

Using the curved needle, slipstitch the lining in place inside the bag. Work blanket stitch (*see* p.121) around the outer edges of the bag and then around both inside edges of the handle **(F)**. Pin on the corsage.

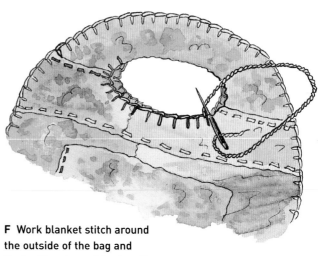

F Work blanket stitch around the outside of the bag and the inside edges of the handle.

MAKING THE DOLL'S BODY

Cut up each side of the glove, retaining one side of the cuff intact and the two middle fingers as "legs" (G). Turn the glove inside out. Stitch up the open edges along both sides, leaving openings for inserting the arms. Turn right side out.

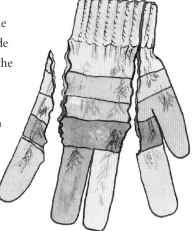

G Cut up the glove to make the body.

MAKING THE DOLL'S HEAD

Wrap a piece of the sock around the spun-paper ball and secure with a few stitches. Stitch the head securely into the collar on the body. Stitch the doll's facial features, securing the thread on the top of the doll's head. Plait the bouclé yarn for the hair. Stitch the plait on top of the doll's head (I).

I Attach the plait of hair.

MAKING THE ARMS AND LEGS

Wrap and glue a piece of fleecy felt around the chenille stem. Insert the chenille stem through the armholes in the body. Stitch the arms in place, turning in the raw edges of the glove. Turn over the glove cuff to form a collar (H). Machine stitch up beyond the fingers to suggest legs.

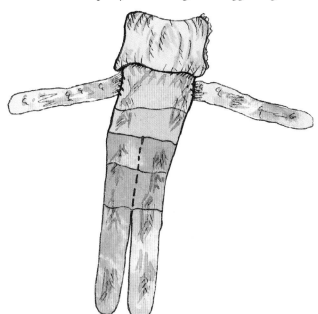

H Insert the arms and turn down the cuff to form a collar.

STYLING THE DOLL

Wrap the plaited yarn around the doll's head to make a topknot, and stitch it in place (J). Make the clothes and handbag from scraps of felt, ribbon, a bead, and a button. Stitch across the fingers of the glove to suggest feet.

J Style the hair and add the clothes and accessories.

Sunday Best Shopper

Elegant yet breezy, with light and airy fabric and pretty detailing, this practical tote is at home in town or country, boardroom or beach.

Textured contemporary lining complements ribbed vintage face fabric

Disciplined, graphic shape looks clean and crisp

Vintage bark cloth is fresh in a sprightly floral pattern

Self-coloured topstitching adds subtle definition

Sunday Best Shopper

Oh the trials of being a celeb! Cameras trained on your front door as you emerge bleary-eyed on a Sunday morning to nip out for papers and milk. Those skimpy plastic bags from the corner shop are not only liable to send your cargo spinning pavement-bound, but look sooooo bad when the paparazzi pics hit the newsstands. The solution is to throw on big shades, catch your hair up in an "I'll-deal-with-you-later" chignon, pick up this gorgeous Grace Kelly-inspired bag, and the columnists will fall over themselves trying to work out where you got it. Get your own back – don't tell 'em!

Materials/Cutting List

Face fabric
front and back: 2 pieces 41x32cm (16x12½in)
sides: 2 pieces 14x32cm (5½x12½in)
base: 41x14cm (16x5½in)
handles: 2 pieces 50x8cm (20x3in)

Firm fusible interfacing
front and back: 2 pieces 41x32cm (16x12½in)
sides: 2 pieces 14x32cm (5½x12½in)
base: 41x14cm (16x5½in)
handles: 2 pieces 50x8cm (20x3¼in)

Lining fabric
front and back: 2 pieces 41x32cm (16x12½in)
sides: 2 pieces 14x32cm (5½x12½in)
base: 41x14cm (16x5½in)

Sewing thread to tone with face and lining fabrics

Grosgrain ribbon 45cmx1.5cm (18inx½in) wide

Straw ribbon or other contrasting ribbon: 45cmx1.5cm (18inx½in) wide

Brooch finding and/or hair bobble optional

Rose
lining fabric: 11x40cm (4½x16in)
floral fabric: 6.5x37cm (2½x14½in)

For each leaf
lining fabric: 8x8cm (3¼x3¼in)
floral fabric: 8x8cm (3¼x3¼in)

ATTACHING THE INTERFACING TO THE BAG

Iron the interfacing onto the wrong side of all the face fabric pieces for the main bag. Pin, baste, and stitch the top, back, and two side pieces together, right sides facing, and stitch up to the top seam allowance. Pin, baste, and stitch the base in position, trimming the corners of the seam allowance as necessary. Press the seams open. Leave the top edge open **(A)**.

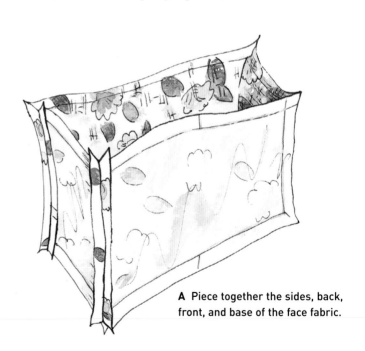

A Piece together the sides, back, front, and base of the face fabric.

A fabric rose stitched onto a brooch fitting, with a hair bobble attached, can be unpinned from the bag and used as a corsage or hair accessory.

Frayed edges inject a light-hearted exuberance.

Duotone lining in green/black echoes the soft, muddied colour of the leaves on the face fabric and really unifies the look.

Grosgrain ribbon and bows made of hat straw provide textural richness.

MAKING THE LINING

Sew together the pieces for the lining as for the main bag, but omitting the interfacing and leaving an opening for turning in the middle of one side seam. Leave the lining wrong side out.

MAKING THE HANDLES

Fold one piece of handle fabric in half lengthwise, right sides facing. Pin, baste, and stitch around the raw edges, leaving an opening for turning. Turn right side out and baste the opening closed. Topstitch all around, 3mm (⅛in) from the edge. Repeat for the second handle.

ASSEMBLING THE BAG

Attach the handles and the lining to the bag following the instructions for a basic lined tote (*see* p.118) **(B)**. Turn the bag right side out and topstitch all the seams. Use a top thread that tones with the face fabric and a bobbin thread that tones with the lining.

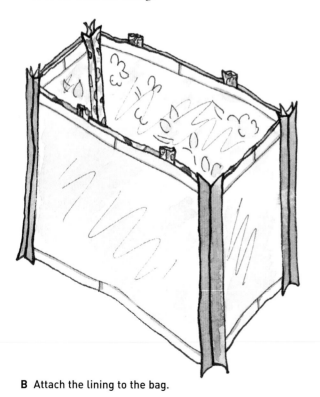

B Attach the lining to the bag.

MAKING THE LINING FOR THE ROSE CORSAGE

Fold the lining fabric in half lengthwise, right sides facing. Stitch diagonally across the folded fabric, starting 2cm (¾in) above the fold at one end. Cut away the excess fabric **(C)**. Turn right side out.

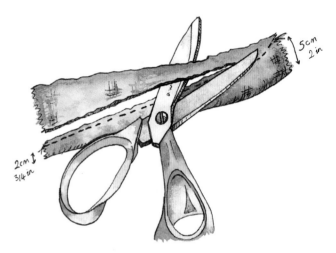

C Trim excess fabric from the seam.

ATTACHING THE FLORAL FABRIC TO THE ROSE

Place the floral fabric on top of the lining fabric tube. Fray the edges of the floral fabric around the edges of the lining. Tuck in the raw ends at the narrow end of the tube and, catching in the floral fabric too, fold the end over so it is level with the bottom seam. Using a doubled thread for strength, secure the end with running stitch **(D)**.

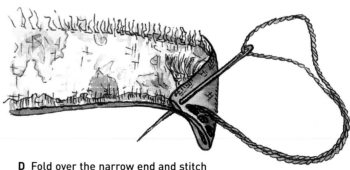

D Fold over the narrow end and stitch the lining and floral fabric down.

FINISHING THE ROSE

Roll the fabrics around the folded end to form the centre of the rose and secure with a stitch. Work a few running stitches along the bottom seam and pull the fabric into gathers before securing it with another stitch. Continue to gather and secure the fabric until you have a pleasing rose shape (E).

ATTACHING THE CORSAGE

Stitch the leaves and flower onto the bag, adding bows of straw and grosgrain ribbon as desired. Alternatively, assemble the corsage and secure it with thread onto a brooch finding and/or hair bobble so that it can be detached and used as a separate accessory.

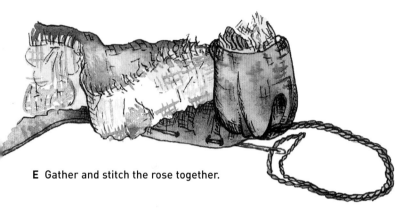

E Gather and stitch the rose together.

MAKING THE LEAVES

Place a piece of floral fabric on top of a piece of lining fabric, wrong sides facing. Draw a leaf shape and stitch around this. Using a pin, fray the fabric back to the stitch line (F). Make one or two more leaves in the same way.

F Fray the edge of the leaf fabric
using a pin.

Wild & Woolly Rag Rug Bag

Forget crochet! Rag rugging is the "new knitting", and is utterly addictive. While you make it, this bag will sit as warm and soothingly as a cat snuggled into your lap.

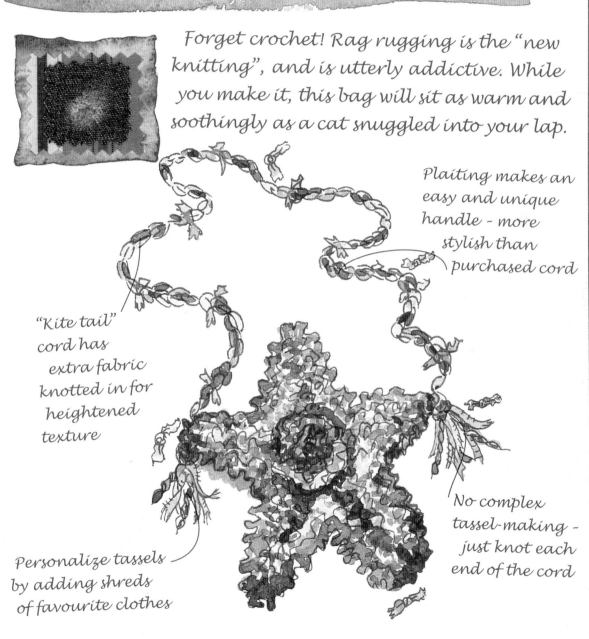

Plaiting makes an easy and unique handle - more stylish than purchased cord

"Kite tail" cord has extra fabric knotted in for heightened texture

No complex tassel-making - just knot each end of the cord

Personalize tassels by adding shreds of favourite clothes

Wild & Woolly Rag Rug Bag

I've always wanted to try my hand at rag rugging, but the realities of my busy life as a working mum somehow never proved compatible with my *Little House on the Prairie* lifestyle fantasies. Until now! At Christmas I spotted the most darling little star- and heart-shaped rag rugs adorning a mantelshelf as garland decorations. My heart leapt with excitement at the sheer attainability of producing something on such a diminutive scale. Having made my first, doll-sized rug after years of prevarication, I naturally wanted to show it off all year round, not just in December. This deliciously scrunchy yet soft bag is worn close to the body and feels as warm as a hug, protective as an amulet. I'm sure it would even protect me from the bears if Pa had to go out a-huntin', Prairie-style!

MATERIALS/CUTTING LIST

Hessian 50x50cm (20x20in)
Marker pen
Embroidery hoop 35cm (14in) diam.
Rag and paper yarns in blue, light blue, cream, grey, black, grey/black, blue/green, or own choice
Large crochet hook
Assorted woolly yarns in red/white mix, blue/white mix, black, or own choice
Assorted cotton textured yarns in dark red, or own choice
Latex adhesive and sturdy card for spreading
Denim 3 pieces 30x30cm (12x12in)
Fusible web 30x30cm (12x12in)
Buckram or pelmet stiffener 30x30cm (12x12in)
Curved needle
Sewing thread to match denim and lining fabric
Lining fabric 2 pieces 30x30cm (12x12in)
Firm iron-on interlining 2 pieces 30x30cm (12x12in)
Denim scraps torn into strips approx. 1.5cm (½in) wide
SEE PAGE 123 FOR TEMPLATE
Enlarge template to 126%, using a photocopier if necessary

STARTING THE RUG FABRIC

Draw the star onto the hessian using the template. Stretch the hessian in the hoop. Loop one end of a length of grey/black rag between your thumb and forefinger and hold this beneath the hoop. Using your other hand, push the hook down through the hessian from the top on the star outline. Catch the loop with the hook **(A)**. Pull the hook and loop back through to the top so there is a cut end of rag on the surface of the hessian.

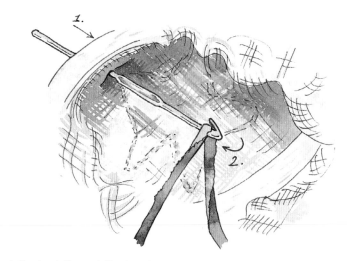

A Push the hook through the hessian (1.) and pick up the loop of rag (2.).

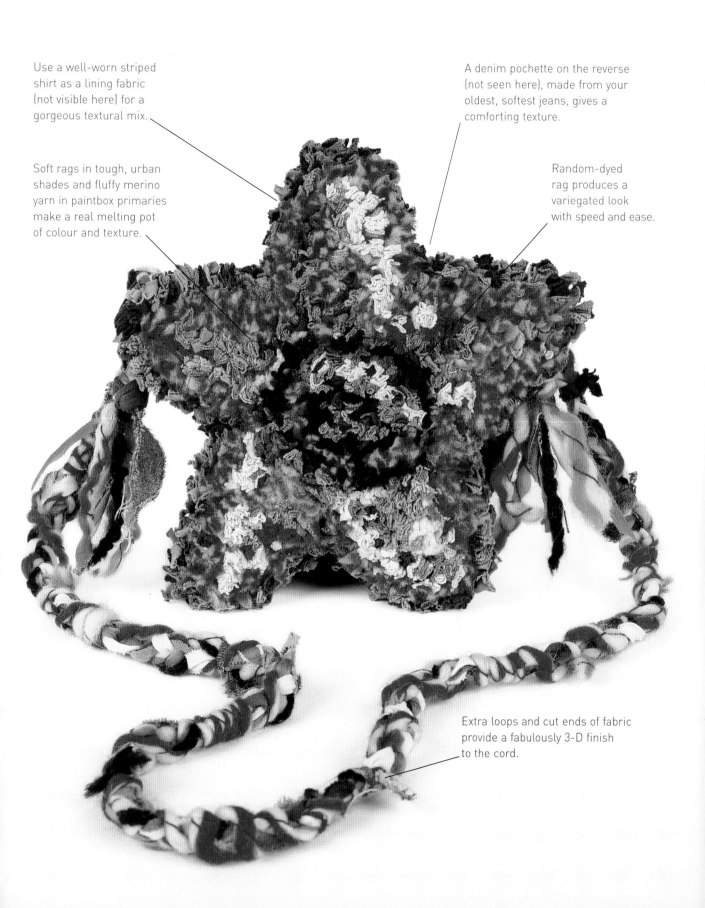

Use a well-worn striped shirt as a lining fabric (not visible here) for a gorgeous textural mix.

Soft rags in tough, urban shades and fluffy merino yarn in paintbox primaries make a real melting pot of colour and texture.

A denim pochette on the reverse (not seen here), made from your oldest, softest jeans, gives a comforting texture.

Random-dyed rag produces a variegated look with speed and ease.

Extra loops and cut ends of fabric provide a fabulously 3-D finish to the cord.

FORMING THE STAR OUTLINE

One or two threads of hessian along the outline from the first entry point (see previous page), push the hook through the hessian again and pick up the next loop of rag. Pull this loop up to the surface and leave it approx. 2.5cm (1in) long. Keep the "stitches" even on the wrong side. Continue, bringing any ends of rag to the top surface (B). Complete the outline. Using sharp shears, holding them flat across the work, trim the loops to approx. 1.5cm (½in).

B Outline the star shape with the loops of rag yarn.

FILLING IN THE STAR

One or two threads of hessian inside the outline, work a row of red/white yarn loops (C). Trim these as before.

C Fill in the second row with red/white yarn.

FINISHING THE DESIGN

Draw a swirl in the centre of the star and work this in black rag loops. Trim the loops. Fill in the rest of the design with the remaining rags and yarns. Trim the loops (D).

D Trim the loops as the design is filled in.

CUTTING OUT THE STAR SHAPE

Remove the hessian from the hoop. Cut out the star leaving a 2.5cm (1in) border around it. Apply adhesive to the wrong side of the hessian (E). Leave for five minutes before pressing the raw edges onto the adhesive; turn under the points of the star first, followed by the sides. Leave the design to dry.

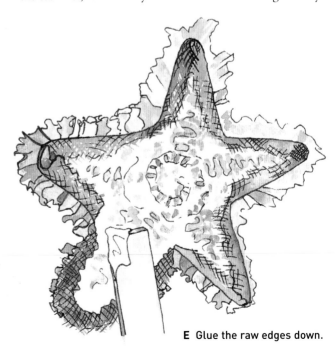

E Glue the raw edges down.

BACKING THE STAR OUTLINE

Place the rug fabric right side down on a flat surface and put a sheet of paper on top. Trace around the outline of the hessian star to make a new template. Cut a second star shape from the denim, using the new template but adding a 1.5cm (½in) seam allowance. Back the denim with fusible web. Cut the buckram to the same size as the new template. Bond the denim to the buckram, following the web manufacturer's directions. Neatly turn the raw edges of the denim over the edges of the buckram and press. Slipstitch the covered buckram onto the back of the rug fabric, wrong sides facing, using the curved needle **(F)**.

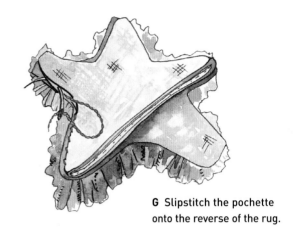

G Slipstitch the pochette onto the reverse of the rug.

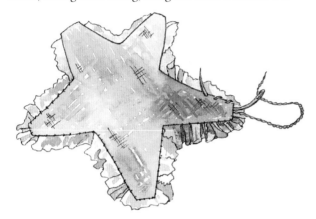

F Slipstitch the denim-covered buckram to the reverse of the rug.

MAKING THE CORD FOR THE HANDLE

Take six 2m (80in) lengths of yarn and rag, knotting pieces together if necessary to create the desired length. Knot the lengths together at one end, leaving a 7.5cm (3in) loose end to form a tassel. Tie the knotted end onto a door handle or other fixed point. Divide the yarn into three groups of two strands and plait them together, knotting the other end of the cord and leaving a second 7.5cm (3in) tassel. Stitch, knot, and tie additional scraps of denim, yarn, and rag randomly along the cord for added texture **(H)**. Stitch the knot of each tassel onto opposite sides of the bag on its reverse.

MAKING THE POCHETTE

Make a template for the pochette by cutting one of the points of the star off the previous template and adding 1.5cm (½in) seam allowance to the cut edge. Using the template, cut out two pieces of lining fabric and two pieces of denim. Back the fabric with fusible interfacing. Pin, baste, and stitch around the outline of the denim, leaving the straight edge open. Trim and press the seams. Repeat the process for the lining, but leave an opening along one edge of the star for turning. Pin, baste, and stitch the denim and lining together around the straight edge. Press the seam, turn right side out, and slipstitch the opening closed. Slipstitch the pochette in place on the reverse of the rug fabric using the curved needle **(G)**.

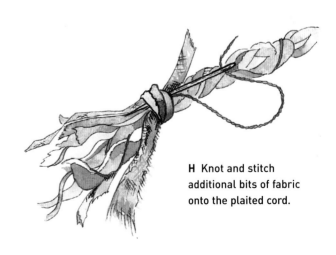

H Knot and stitch additional bits of fabric onto the plaited cord.

Vintage Scarf Bag

Silkily voluptuous vintage scarves still turn up in thrift shops, or may be your cherished heirlooms. Here's a great way to let them take centre stage again.

Antiqued-brass D rings nod to a certain equestrian-influenced fashion house

Raid the dressing-up box for scraps with which to accessorize

Matt, Indian sequins give a dustily well-travelled look

Pockets from a favourite coat mean no need for buttonholing.

Mélange of glossy satin, matt corduroy, and tweed is highly tactile

Vintage Scarf Bag

I am an inveterate hoarder, especially of fabrics, but am also a recent convert to de-junking. This project proved a perfect combination of such seemingly opposing passions as it gave me the perfect excuse to trawl through my collection and actually give my treasured scraps the new lease of life I had always envisaged for them. It is hugely satisfying to transform not only recycled fabrics but also their associated memories into something wearable and useful. Helping an equally textile-addicted friend de-junk her attic, we came across an ancient box of dressing-up clothes, which yielded the red taffeta cummerband I chopped up to make the looped scarf. As a result, this bag is a sort of 3-D scrapbook, not only of our individual lives but also, with its intertwined nature, of our friendship. For me, that adds enormously to the bag's appeal.

MATERIALS/CUTTING LIST

Fabrics in contrasting textures to make patchwork 30x38cm (12x15in)
Pattern graph paper
Firm iron-on interfacing 2 pieces 30x38cm (12x15in)
Fusible web
Beads, sequins, ribbons, and trim as desired
Corduroy for back of bag 30x38cm (12x15in)
Sewing thread to match fabrics
Satin lining fabric: 2 pieces 30x38cm (12x15in)
Old belt for the handle
2 bronze-effect D rings to suit size of belt
Scarf to decorate handle

CREATING THE FACE FABRIC

Draw a 30x38cm (12x15in) rectangle on the graph paper. Working on an ironing board, arrange the fabric for the patchwork within the outline on the paper, until you are happy with the result. Place the interfacing shiny side down over the patchwork and securely pin it to all the pieces of fabric, but not the paper. Turn the interfacing and patchwork over and carefully remove the pins. Bond the appliqué with a hot iron **(A)**. Add additional layers of trim using fusible web, and make sure all the raw edges of fabric inside the outline are covered.

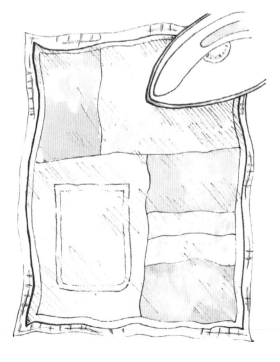

A Iron the patchwork pieces onto the interfacing.

Multi-packs of ribbons and braids, sold for embellishing greetings cards, are great value and often contain imaginative mixes of colour and weave, such as the range of black, neutral, and red used here.

A glossy satin lining adds a fittingly opulent flourish to an already lavish production.

This richly textural, plaited leather-look fabric was originally a waistband from a thrift shop skirt, which also yielded the chocolate-brown corduroy for the reverse side.

Cheat! Sewing beads into the base fabric along a length of ribbon or braid is a great way of attaching trim without leaving stitches visible.

ADDING EMBELLISHMENTS

Turn the pieced fabric right side up. Stitch on any non-ironable trims, such as beads, sequins, or leather-look fabric **(B)**.

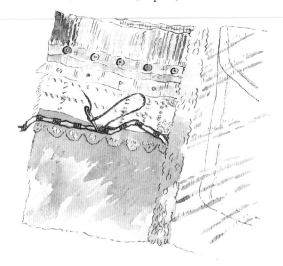

B Stitch on the non-fusible trims.

MAKING THE BAG

Mark seam allowances on the pieced fabric. Pin, baste, and stitch it to the corduroy, backed with interfacing, along the sides and bottom edges, right sides facing and up to the top seam allowance. Clip across the seam allowance at the corners. Turn the bag right side out.

MAKING THE LINING

Make the lining in the same way as the main bag, but leave a generous opening along one side for turning. Clip the corners. Leave the lining wrong side out **(C)**.

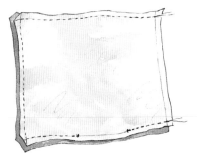

C Stitch the lining pieces together, right sides facing, leaving an opening for turning.

MAKING THE D-RING LOOPS

Cut two 14cm (5½in) lengths from the belt. Fold each piece in half lengthwise and topstitch along the length to secure the edges. Fold the remainder of the belt in half lengthwise and topstitch it in the same way. Thread each short length of belt through a D-ring and fold it in half to make a loop. Aligning the raw ends, pin and baste these D-ring loops in place, one at the top right edge of the bag front, the other on the top right edge of the reverse of the bag, so there is a loop on each side of the bag. Stitch the loops just inside the seam allowance to secure them **(D)**.

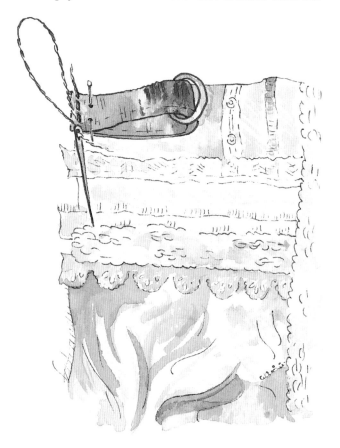

D Attach the D-ring loops to the bag.

ATTACHING THE LINING

Place the bag inside the lining, right sides facing. Pin, baste, and stitch around the top edge of the bag (E). Clip across the seam allowance at the top corners. Turn the bag right side out and slipstitch the opening in the lining seam closed.

ADDING THE HANDLE AND FINISHING TOUCHES

Thread each end of the remaining long length of belt through the D-rings to make the handle. Fold under the raw ends and stitch them securely in place (F). Loop a scarf through one end of the handle for decoration.

E Stitch the lining around the top edge of the bag, right sides facing.

F Attach the handle to the D-ring loops.

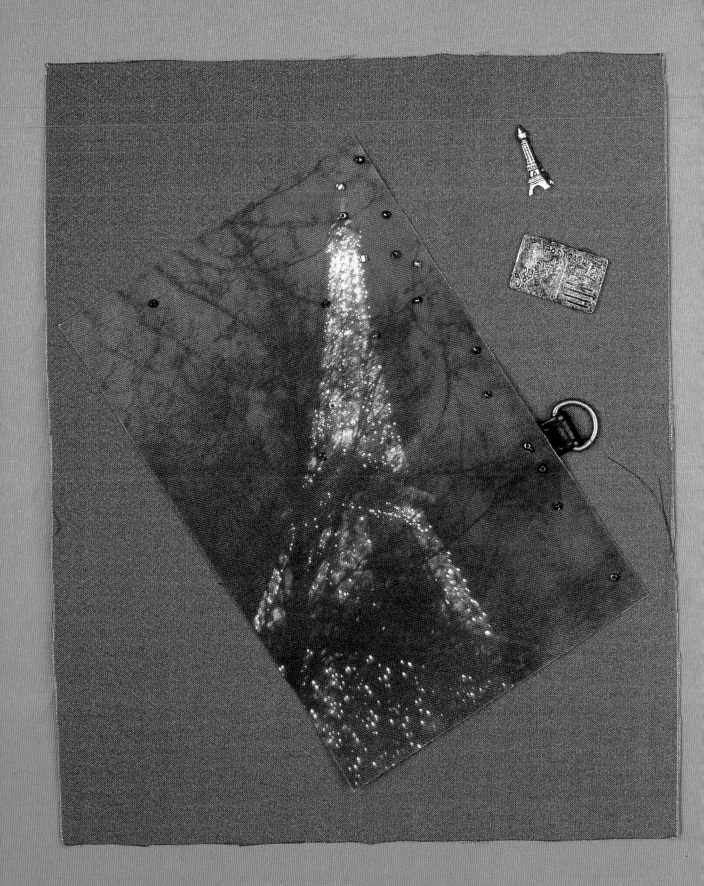

Picture Postcard Purse

Commemorate special moments on this chic purse – it doesn't have to be a glamorous location to be meaningful to you.

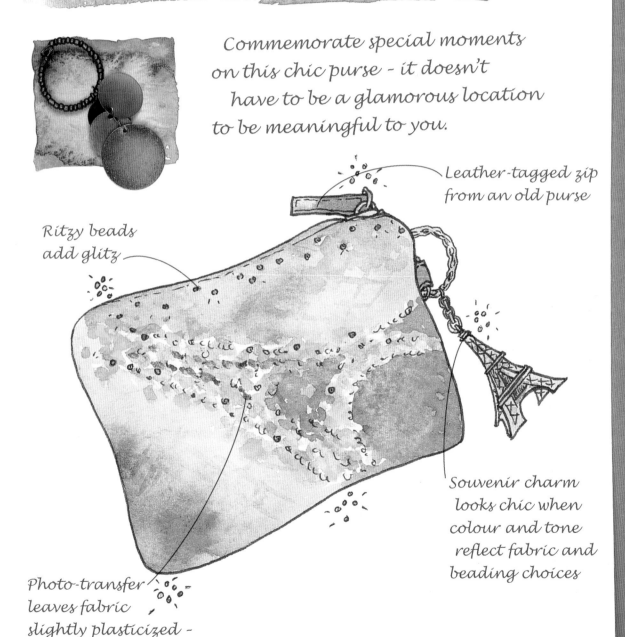

Leather-tagged zip from an old purse

Ritzy beads add glitz

Souvenir charm looks chic when colour and tone reflect fabric and beading choices

Photo-transfer leaves fabric slightly plasticized – sheeny and practical

Picture Postcard Purse

Who would have thought that this sophisticated bijou pochette started life as a seen-better-days white(ish!) pillowcase? Transferring photos to fabric is a great way to get those treasured holiday snaps off your digital camera and out there into your everyday life. It's not the least bit technical. Just take your disc, a print out, or snapshot to any copy shop, and they will print the image onto fabric. I used an old pillowcase, partly because well-washed white cotton works really well as a base fabric for photo transfer, and partly because the parsimonious part of me gets a big feel-good buzz out of recycling. Charity shops often yield pillowcases for just a few pence, making this purse economical as well as ecologically sound.

MATERIALS/CUTTING LIST

Face fabric white cotton fabric 18x13cm (7x5in), with transferred photo image (service available at copy shops)
Assorted tiny beads to tone with photo image
Sewing thread to match fabrics
Fabric/suedette for zip ends, 2.5x5cm (1x2in), to tone with photo image
Zip 15cm (6in)
Fabric/suedette for reverse side, 18x13cm (7x5in), to tone with photo image
Satin lining 2 pieces 18x13cm (7x5in) in toning shade
Charm or keyring
Tagged mini D ring
YOU WILL NEED ACCESS TO A COPY SHOP FOR COPYING IMAGES TO FABRIC

CREATING THE FACE FABRIC

Take your chosen photograph to a copy shop to have it transferred onto the white fabric. Before you start to make the bag, accentuate selected areas of the transferred image by stitching on beads **(A)**.

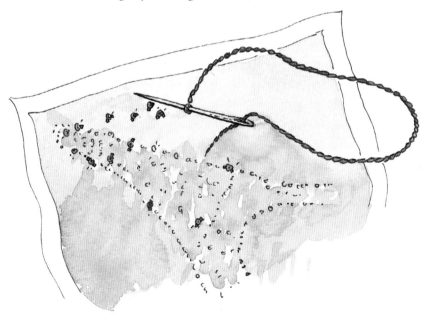

A Embellish the image with beads.

A scrap from an old, worn scarf yields a rich, nut-brown satin lining (not visible).

Old suedette, recycled from a skirt, forms the reverse side for an interesting mix of texture.

A D-ring, complete with leather strap, came from a spectacularly nasty purse that cost pennies in a factory-outlet bargain bin (rich pickings for fabrics and haberdashery)!

Wine-glass charms often turn up very inexpensively in post-Christmas sales and are far too ritzy to save only for their original purpose.

INSERTING THE ZIP

Fold each piece of fabric for the zip ends in half, wrong sides facing, to form a square. Baste one zip end to each end of the zip, folded edges toward the zip opening. Turn the seam allowance along the top edge of the face fabric towards the wrong side and press. In the same way, turn under the seam allowance on the fabric that will form the reverse of the purse. Baste the wrong side of each piece of fabric to the right side of the zip tape (do not use pins as these may mark the transferred image) **(B)**.

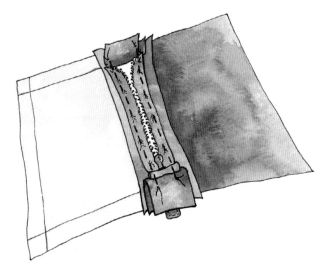

B Baste the zip to the face fabric.

ADDING THE LINING

Turn under and press the seam allowance along one long edge of each piece of lining fabric. Baste and slipstitch the lining pieces in place along the zip tape, wrong sides facing, and make sure the stitches do not show through on the right side.

TOPSTITCHING THE ZIP

Working on the right side, topstitch through all the layers of the fabrics and lining on each side of the zip tape **(C)**.

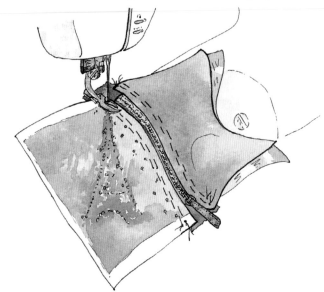

C Topstitch the face fabric and lining to the zip.

ASSEMBLING THE PURSE

Baste the tag on the D-ring to the right side of the face fabric halfway down one of the side seams, inside the seam allowance, and aligning the raw edges. Open the zip. Baste and stitch the two face fabrics together around the raw edges, right sides facing. Repeat for the lining, leaving an opening in the bottom edge for turning **(D)**.

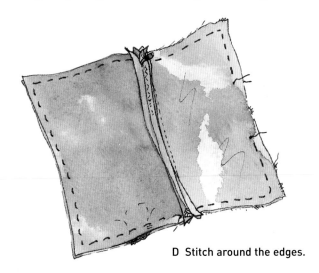

D Stitch around the edges.

FINISHING THE PURSE

Turn the purse right side out. Slipstitch the opening in the lining closed **(E)**. Push the lining into the main purse. Attach the charm to the D-ring.

E Slipstitch the lining closed.

Baby Changing Bag

Brighter-than-bright fabric makes
for one groovy baby; or change
the size of the mat and it's a workout
bag for gym bunnies.

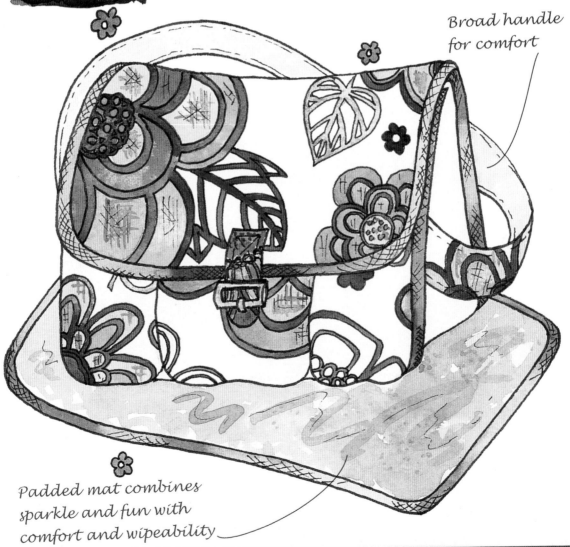

Broad handle
for comfort

Padded mat combines
sparkle and fun with
comfort and wipeability

Baby Changing Bag

With babies being the latest must-have accessory, designers have been quick to cash in on the trend with colourful bags to carry all that necessary baby paraphernalia in style. However, such style comes at a price few can afford, given the expenses that come with each stork. This funky bag uses only a small amount of inexpensive cotton furnishing fabric to create just as slick an impression for a fraction of the cost. The changing mat inside is inspired and highly practical, with its wipe-clean surface.

MATERIALS/CUTTING LIST

Face fabric
back, top, and flap: 38x58cm (15x23in)
front: 38x29cm (15x11½in)
pocket: 71x28cm (28x11in)
sides and base: 90x21cm (35½x8¼in)
buckle strap: 2 pieces 6x15cm (2¼x6in)
strap: 130x8cm (51x3¼in)
mat: 32x65cm (12½x25½in)

Lining
back, top, and flap: 38x58cm (15x23in)
front: 38x29cm (15x11½in)
pocket: 71x28cm (28x11in)
sides and base: 90x21cm (35½x8¼in)

Firm iron-on interfacing
back, top, and flap: 38x58cm (15x23in)
front: 38x29cm (15x11½in)
pocket: 71x28cm (28x11in)
sides and base: 90x21cm (35½x8¼in)

Sewing thread to match fabrics
Blue denim 7mx8cm (7½ydx3¼in) for
bias binding
Buckle
Small eyelet
Sewing machine needle for plastic fabric
PVC-coated cotton fabric in pink sparkle
32x65cm (12½x25½in)
Medium-weight synthetic wadding
32x65cm (12½x25½in)

SEE PAGE 124 FOR TEMPLATE

Enlarge template to 346%, using a photo-copier if necessary. Mark out fabric pieces on the right side except for the pocket, which needs to be marked out on both sides

PREPARING THE FABRIC

Cut the pocket out of the face and lining fabrics, using the template. Mark and cut identical rounded corners on one short end of the back, top, and flap face panel to shape the flap. Repeat for the lining. Iron the interfacing onto the reverse of all the face fabric panels. Transfer the pattern markings to the right side of all the panels, and also to the wrong side of the pocket panel. Stitch around the seam lines to reinforce them.

LINING THE POCKET

Pin, baste, and stitch the face and lining fabrics of the pocket together along the top edge, right sides facing **(A)**. Turn right side out. Pin, baste, and stitch, matching up the A, B, C, and D letters on the template (*see* p124) to form the pockets.

A Stitch the bottom edges of the fabric together to form the pockets.

Contrast binding in a marled weave picks up the grain of the face fabric and its mottled colour means it won't show dirt as quickly as a flat, pale shade.

A deep flap with ornamental buckle means there's no need for fixings. Easy to make, and mega-fast access in a nappy-changing crisis.

Binding all the edges means that this bag is tough enough to withstand the rough and tumble of a parent's daily life.

LINING AND BINDING THE PANELS

Baste the lining to the face fabric for all the other panels, wrong sides facing. Make the binding (*see* p.118). Apply binding to the top edge of the front panel and the short edges of the side and base panel. Matching the centre points, bind the front edge of the flap, leaving long ends of approximately 90cm (36in) **(B)**.

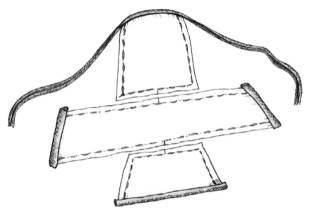

B Baste the lining onto the panels and add binding.

ATTACHING THE POCKET

Pin and baste the pocket to the front panel, aligning the bottom and side edges. Pin, baste, and stitch along the pocket divisions, spacing them at even intervals across the front panel **(C)**.

C Stitch the pocket to the front panel.

MAKING AND ATTACHING THE STRAP

Fold the strap fabric in half lengthwise, right sides facing. Pin, baste, and stitch around the outside edges, leaving an opening in the long edge for turning. Turn the strap right side out and baste the opening closed. Topstitch all around the strap, 3mm (⅛in) from the edge. Baste each end of the strap centrally and 11cm (4¼in) down from the bound top edge on each end of the side panel. Topstitch a rectangle to secure each end of the strap, and then stitch diagonally across this in both directions to give the strap additional strength **(D)**.

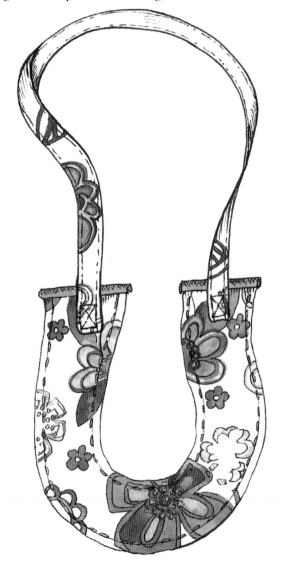

D Attach the strap securely to the side panel.

ASSEMBLING THE BAG

Pin and baste the side and base panel to the front panel, wrong sides facing, and make sure the top bound edges align. Attach the back panel in the same way. Stitch the seams **(E)**.

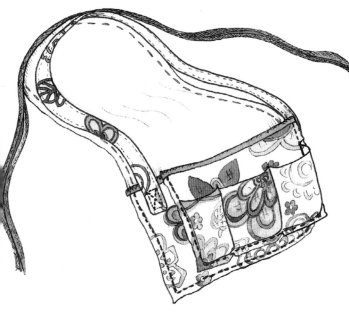

E Stitch the panels together.

FINISHING THE BINDING

Apply binding around the side and bottom raw edges of the front panel, neatly turning the ends under. Continue binding around the flap, down the back side seams, around the bottom corners, and across the back panel. Turn under and secure the end in the middle of the back edge.

MAKING AND APPLYING THE BUCKLED STRAP

Cut one short end of both pieces of fabric for the buckled strap to produce a curve. Pin, baste, and stitch the fabric for the buckled strap together, right sides facing, and leave the short, straight end open for turning. Trim the seam allowance to 3mm (⅛in). Turn the strap right side out and press. Following the manufacturer's directions, apply one or two eyelets. Slip the buckle onto the strap and fasten it in one of the eyelets. Stitch the buckled strap, centred on the front flap, in the same way as the main strap **(F)**.

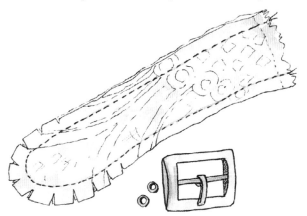

F Make the buckled strap.

MAKING THE MAT

Layer the PVC-coated fabric, right side down, with the wadding and face fabric on top, right side up. Baste and stitch together within the seam allowance. Bind around the edges of the mat, turning the end under **(G)**. Use a slightly longer stitch than usual to avoid tearing the fabric.

G Add binding to the edges of the mat.

Miss Havisham's Evening Bag

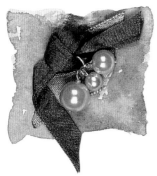

Gorgeous fabric, lace, buttons, and beads can often be salvaged at a fraction of couture prices from sale rails, outlet stores, or car boot (garage) sales. This bag provides an excuse to use these treasures and express your maximalist tendencies.

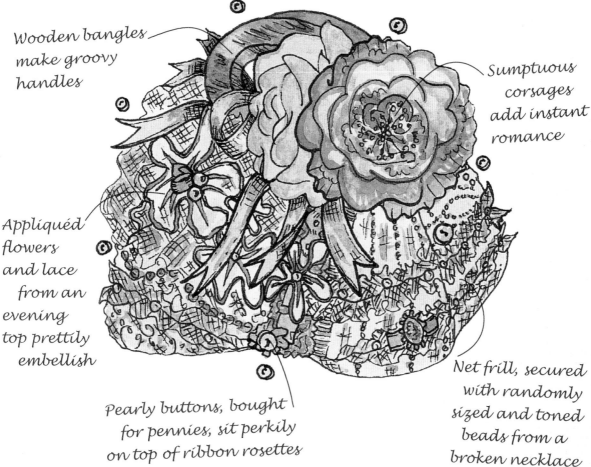

Wooden bangles make groovy handles

Sumptuous corsages add instant romance

Appliquéd flowers and lace from an evening top prettily embellish

Pearly buttons, bought for pennies, sit perkily on top of ribbon rosettes

Net frill, secured with randomly sized and toned beads from a broken necklace

Miss Havisham's Evening Bag

After years in first Goth-inspired, then Japanese minimalist black, the lure of boudoir chic finally got the better of me. All those frills, fripperies, and the sheer delight of – whisper the word – "prettiness", after decades in sleek monochrome, spoke volumes to my inner Scarlett O'Hara. Boudoir chic, like Miss Havisham's wedding-day finery, doesn't get much of a public airing, so I made this darling little confection in subdued lingerie shades as a way of bringing a little romance out of the bedroom and into everyday life.

MATERIALS/CUTTING LIST

Satin face fabric
front and back: 2 pieces 30x23cm (12x9in)
sides and base: 11x67cm (4¼x26½in)
Firm iron-on interfacing 4 pieces 30x23cm
(12x9in); 1 piece 11x67cm (4¼x26½in)
Lace face fabric
front and back: 2 pieces 30x23cm (12x9in)
sides and base: 11x67cm (4¼x26½in)
Assorted fabric scraps e.g. frills from net
petticoats, appliqué motifs, organza with
beading, sequinned netting, and brocade
shoulder straps
Assorted haberdashery scraps e.g. ribbon,
lace, sequins, pearly buttons, and odd
beads in varying sizes and textures
Sewing thread to match face fabric and
trimmings
Silk or rayon ribbon for rosettes,
2 lengths 30cmx12mm (12x½in) wide
Bangles 2 for handles (or purchased
handles)
Assorted trinkets e.g. cameo brooches,
ribbon-trimmed hair slides, and pearls
Satin lining
front and back: 2 pieces 30x23cm (12x9in)
sides and base: 11x67cm (4½x26½in)
Silk or rayon ribbon for ties,
8 lengths 60cmx12mm (24x½in) wide
Flower brooches 2

DECORATING THE FACE FABRIC

Fuse the interfacing to the wrong side of the face fabric pieces. Mark out the seam allowances and centre of each edge on both sides of the fabric. Pin and baste the lace fabric over all the pieces of face fabric, aligning the edges. Pin and baste the net, appliqué motifs, and organza on the front and side panels. When you are happy with the design, stitch the trimmings in place **(A)**.

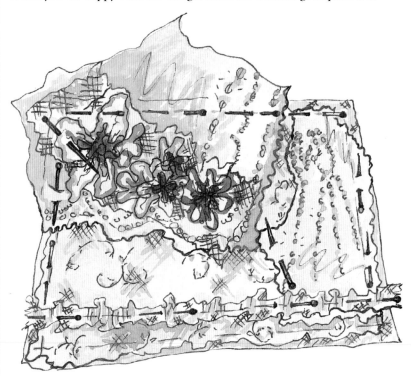

A Layer lace fabric, then net, organza, and appliqué motifs on the face fabric.

Broken jewellery is heartbreaking to discard, especially when it has sentimental associations. Pin or stitch it in place here to appease your guilt and your decorative impulses simultaneously.

Last season's Maharishi pants in khaki satin make a surprisingly empathetic lining. The pull-up ties from the legs are given new lives as decorative ribbons.

Floppy rayon ribbons tumble and cascade prettily over the bag rather than sticking out awkwardly as jaunty satin might – more "Greta Garbo in **Camille"** than "Shirley Temple on the **Good Ship Lollipop"**.

Hair slides and jewellery can often be found cheaply in end-of-season sales because they're slightly damaged or don't suit the new season's look. That doesn't matter in this timeless design. If it's broken, just snap it off and stitch the decorative piece onto the bag.

Chiffon already embellished with iridescent sequins gives a labour-intensive look – without the labour.

ADDING DETAILS TO THE FABRIC

Pin, baste, and stitch on new or recycled materials, such as strips of lace and ribbon. Secure and trim them with beads and sequins (B).

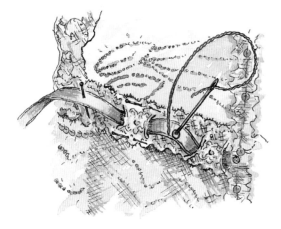

B Thread ribbon through lace and secure with beads.

MAKING THE ROSETTES

Work running stitch along one long edge of the ribbon for each rosette. Gather up the ribbon to give a pleasing shape and secure the thread. Stitching diagonally towards the opposite long edge of the ribbon at each end will make gathering it into a circle even easier. Attach a button to decorate each rosette (C). Stitch the rosettes, and any additional trinkets, on the panel for the bag front.

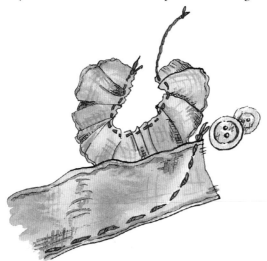

C Gather the rosettes and top each with a button.

ASSEMBLING THE BAG

Pin, baste, and stitch the sides and base panel to the front panel, right sides facing, and align the edges that will make the top of the bag (D). Repeat the process to attach the back panel. Turn the bag right side out.

D Stitch together the front, sides and base panels, and repeat for the back panel.

MAKING THE LINING

Pin, baste, and stitch the lining pieces together in the same way as for the main bag, right sides facing, leaving an opening in one seam for turning. Leave wrong side out.

ATTACHING THE PULL-UP TIES

Fold the eight lengths of ribbon for the ties in half. Baste the folded end of four of the ribbons to the top edge of the front panel, evenly spaced along the edge and well inside the seam allowance (E). Attach the other four ribbons to the back panel in the same way.

E Baste the folded ends of the ribbon ties onto the main bag within the seam allowance.

ATTACHING THE LINING

Place the main bag, and the loose ends of the ties, inside the lining, right sides facing, and align the raw edges around the top. Pin, baste, and stitch the lining to the face fabric around the top edge (F). Turn the bag right side out through the opening in the lining. Slipstitch the opening closed.

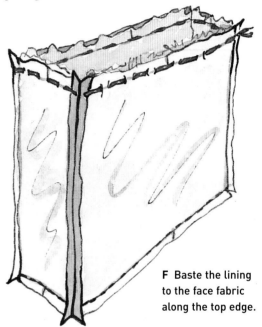

F Baste the lining to the face fabric along the top edge.

ATTACHING THE HANDLES

Tie the ribbons around the handles to secure them in place (G). Pin on the flower corsages.

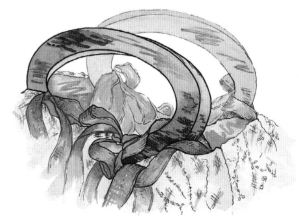

G Tie the ribbons around the handles.

Favourite Clothes Bag

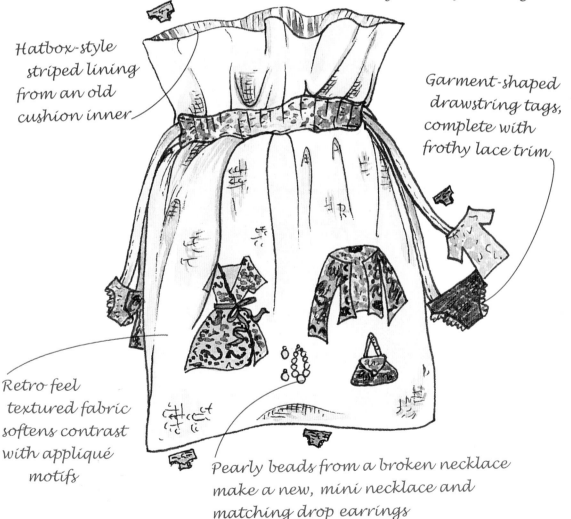

You can adapt this design to suit all sorts of contents - not just laundry. Give it a waterproof lining for swimming gear, a baize lining for shoes, or make smaller, satin-lined versions for jewellery or lingerie.

Hatbox-style striped lining from an old cushion inner

Garment-shaped drawstring tags, complete with frothy lace trim

Retro feel textured fabric softens contrast with appliqué motifs

Pearly beads from a broken necklace make a new, mini necklace and matching drop earrings

Favourite Clothes Bag

I'm a big fan of making the mundane as magical as possible. Time away from the treadmill of everyday life is so precious that everything about a hard-earned weekend away should be exciting – even stowing the laundry. Hopefully, the sweet motifs on this dinky little bag will spark memories of red-letter days as you return to the grind of washing your smalls. A good friend of mine has the perfect word to describe this bag, with its cheeky drawstring tags – "fubsy". Somehow, I know exactly what she means!

MATERIALS/CUTTING LIST

Assorted quilting fabrics for clothes appliqué
Fusible web
Face fabric 2 pieces 35x45cm (14x18in)
Scrap of ribbon 3mm (⅛in) wide
Assorted tiny beads
Stranded embroidery cotton
Sewing thread to match fabrics
Lining fabric 2 pieces 35x45cm (14x18in)
Contrasting fabric for drawstring bands, 2 pieces 33x6cm (13x2¼in)
Contrasting fabric for drawstrings, 2 pieces 1mx4.5cm (40x1¾in)
Short lengths of narrow lace
SEE RIGHT AND PAGE 68 FOR TEMPLATES
Enlarge templates on p68 to 180%, using a photocopier as necessary.

DECORATING THE FACE FABRIC

Following the manufacturer's directions, bond the fusible web to the wrong side of the quilting fabrics. Trace the templates you wish to appliqué onto the main bag **(A)** and **(B)**. Transfer the shapes onto the fabric. Cut out the motifs and fuse them to the face fabric of the bag.

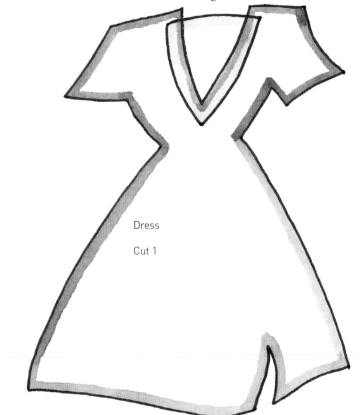

Dress

Cut 1

A Trace the dress template at this size.

Use these appliqué shapes, or sketch motifs from your own favourite clothes.

A contrasting drawstring band is applied to the outside of the bag and makes the construction simplicity itself.

A narrow silk-ribbon handle on the handbag motif gives a soft look, in harmony with the gentle tones of the cotton quilting fabrics.

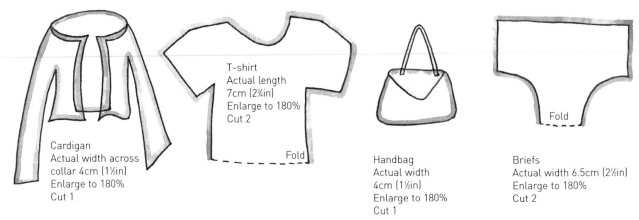

T-shirt
Actual length
7cm (2¾in)
Enlarge to 180%
Cut 2

Fold

Cardigan
Actual width across
collar 4cm (1½in)
Enlarge to 180%
Cut 1

Handbag
Actual width
4cm (1½in)
Enlarge to 180%
Cut 1

Briefs
Actual width 6.5cm (2½in)
Enlarge to 180%
Cut 2

Fold

B Trace the remaining templates at the percentage given.

DECORATING THE MOTIFS

Add hand-stitched detail to the motifs. This could include working embroidery stitches along the front edge of the dress and in simple patterns to enhance the fabric, making a delicate ribbon sash around the waist of the dress (leaving the bow and ends free), and attaching tiny beads as buttons on the cardigan **(C)**. You could also make a tiny pearl necklace and earrings to attach to the bag and complete the "wardrobe".

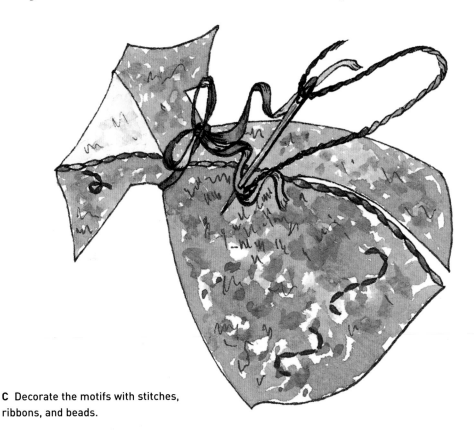

C Decorate the motifs with stitches, ribbons, and beads.

ASSEMBLING THE BAG

Assemble the main bag following the directions for the basic lined tote bag (*see* p.118), but omitting the handles. Then turn the bag right side out and slipstitch the opening closed.

MAKING THE DRAWSTRING BANDS

Take one of the pieces of fabric for the drawstring bands and press the seam allowances along the short edges towards the wrong side. Then press under the seam allowances along the long edges **(D)**. Pin, baste, and topstitch the band onto the front of the bag, 10.5cm (4in) down from the top edge and 1cm (⅜in) in from each side. Take the other piece of fabric, make the second band in the same way, and stitch it to the reverse side of the bag.

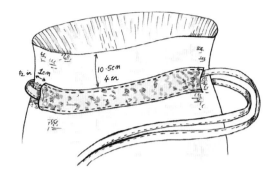

E Thread the first drawstring through the bands.

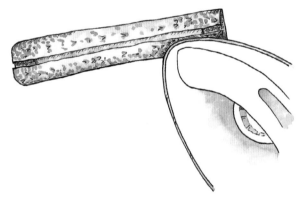

D Press the seam allowances on the drawstring bands towards the centre.

MAKING THE DRAWSTRINGS

Fold one of the pieces of fabric for the drawstrings in half lengthwise with wrong sides facing. Pin, baste, and stitch it together along the long edge. Trim the seam allowance to 3mm (⅛in). Fold the drawstring in half again lengthwise, concealing the seam allowance. Topstitch the long edges together. Make a second drawstring in the same way. Thread one drawstring through first one and then the second band on the bag **(E)**. Thread the other drawstring in the opposite direction, so you have two loose ends on each side of the bag.

MAKING THE DRAWSTRING ENDS

Fold the fabric for the T-shirt and briefs motifs and place the templates on the folds as directed (*see* top of p.68). Cut out two of each motif. To make a T-shirt, fold the fabric along the fold line, right sides facing. Pin, baste, and stitch all around the edges, leaving a short opening along the top of one shoulder. Trim and clip into the seam allowances. Turn right sides out and press the opening edges together. Insert the end of a drawstring into the opening and machine stitch the opening closed. Make a second T-shirt in the same way and attach it to a drawstring on the other side of the bag. Make and attach two pairs of briefs in the same way, adding lace between the layers around the leg openings **(F)**.

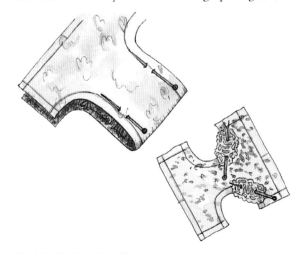

F Make the brief motifs and add lace to the leg openings.

Funky Fruit Bag

This groovy '60s-style reversible bag is ultra quick and simple to make for gals on the go. Print using one half of your apple and juice the other for a healthy smoothie!

Zipadeedoodah bright contrast lining for when the bag is reversed

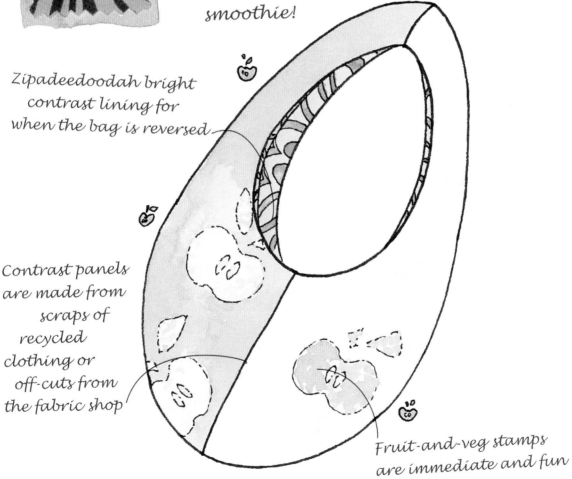

Contrast panels are made from scraps of recycled clothing or off-cuts from the fabric shop

Fruit-and-veg stamps are immediate and fun

Funky Fruit Bag

This bag is as fresh as a daisy, but there's not a flower in sight. The zingy bite here comes from choosing colours and textures that are crisp and clean. The simple fruit stamp on pure cotton fabric is as temptingly simple as a meal served on pure white china. An apple and lime pop-art print makes a zesty lining that comes to the fore when the bag is reversed, providing a totally different look. Experiment with different fruits and vegetables for alternative colourways – peppers in red, emerald, or yellow are tasty possibilities.

MATERIALS/CUTTING LIST

White cotton fabric 2 pieces
30x80cm (12x32in)
Lime green cotton fabric 2 pieces
30x80cm (12x32in)
Lining fabric 2 pieces 30x80cm (12x32in)
Firm iron-on interfacing 4 pieces
30x80cm (12x32in)
Large cooking apple cut in half
Acrylic paint in white and lime green to
match fabric
Plate in a plastic bag to act as a palette
Paint brush
Sponge scouring pad
Sewing thread to match fabrics
SEE PAGE 124 FOR TEMPLATE
Enlarge template to 415%,
using a photocopier as necessary.

PREPARING THE LINING AND FACE FABRICS

Back the lining and face fabrics with interfacing. Mark and cut out the pattern pieces according to the directions on the template. Mark the seam lines on the reverse of each piece.

PRINTING THE APPLES

Brush a scant amount of paint onto the cut surface of the apple **(A)**. Make some test prints on offcuts of fabric before printing the apple shape at random onto the white and green face fabrics.

A Paint the apple ready for stamping.

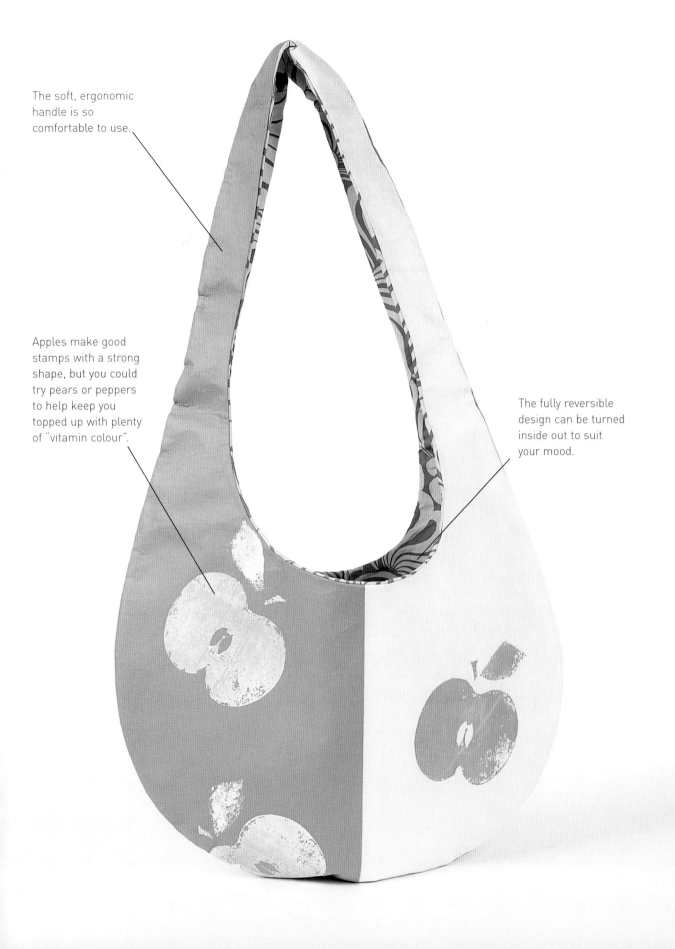

The soft, ergonomic handle is so comfortable to use.

Apples make good stamps with a strong shape, but you could try pears or peppers to help keep you topped up with plenty of "vitamin colour".

The fully reversible design can be turned inside out to suit your mood.

PRINTING LEAVES AND STEMS

Using scissors, cut simple leaf and stem shapes from the sponge of the scouring pad, leaving the scouring part to hold onto **(B)**. Dip the sponge into the paint and dab the excess onto kitchen paper before printing. Make test prints before committing to the face fabric. Press with a hot iron through a muslin pressing cloth to fix the paint.

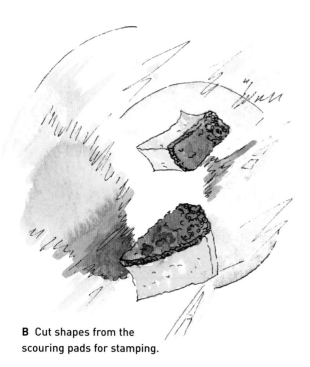

B Cut shapes from the scouring pads for stamping.

MAKING THE FRONT AND BACK PANELS

Pin, baste, and stitch a piece of green and a piece of white face fabric together, right sides facing, along the straight central seam on the main body of the bag to make the front panel. Press the seam open. Repeat to make the back panel.

ASSEMBLING THE BAG

Place the back and front panels together with right sides facing. Pin, baste, and stitch them together around the outer edge of the bag only. Trim the seam allowance to 6mm (¼in) **(C)**. Clip into the seam allowance to allow smooth turning.

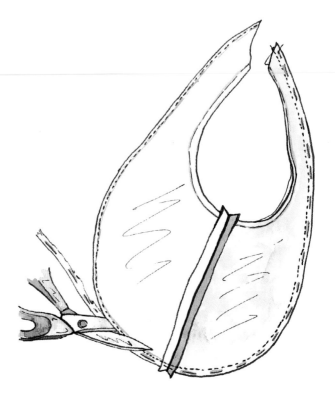

C Join the pieces of the main bag and trim the seam.

MAKING THE LINING

Make the lining in the same way as the main bag **(D)**.

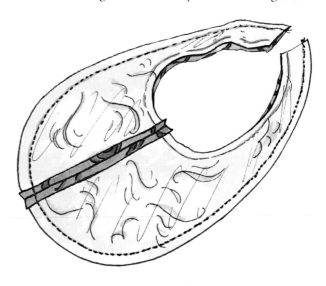

D Assemble the lining and stitch around the outer edge.

ATTACHING THE LINING

Turn the main bag right side out and press the seam open. Place the main bag inside the lining, right sides facing **(E)**. Pin, baste, and stitch the lining and the bag together around the inner curve only. Leave the ends of the handle unstitched and disconnected for turning.

FINISHING THE HANDLE

Carefully turn the bag right side out through the handle. Turn under the raw edge on one side of the handle and place the other side inside it. Neatly slipstitch the two sides of the handle together **(F)**.

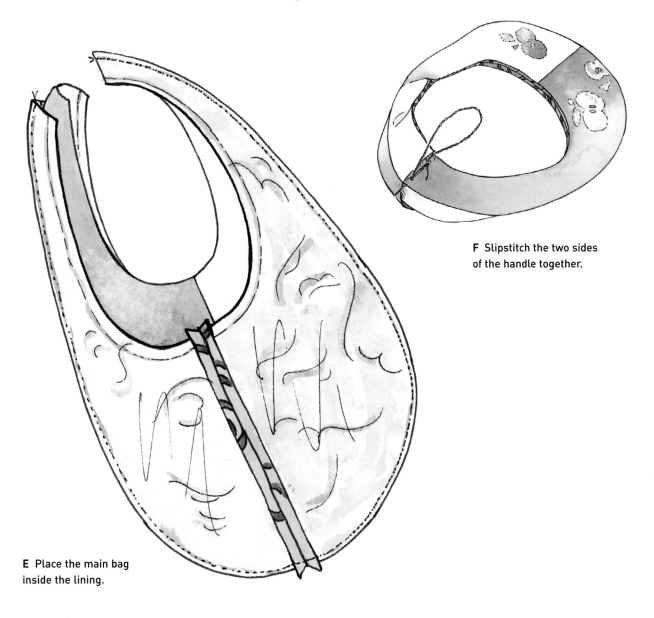

F Slipstitch the two sides of the handle together.

E Place the main bag inside the lining.

Two-Way Polka-Dot Bag

The crisp angularity of this modern classic is softened by the choice of cream ribbed fabric and the addition of yummy polka dots, of which a girl can surely never have too many!

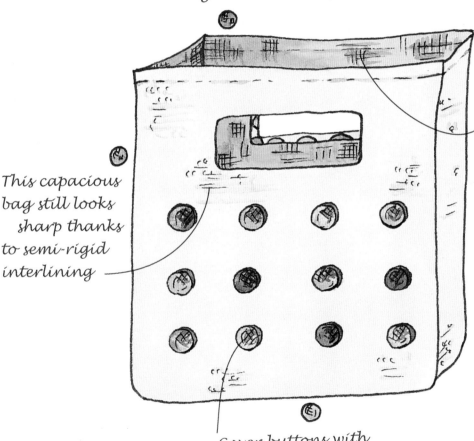

Textured lining fabric gives a retro softness.

This capacious bag still looks sharp thanks to semi-rigid interlining

Cover buttons with off-cuts of face fabric

Two-Way Polka-Dot Bag

Ever since Damien Hirst splashed jumbo-sized polka dots across gallery walls, a car, and even a boat on the Thames, designers have had a renewed love affair with all things spotty. A far cry from the insipid pastel pink and white of the '50s, these babies are "souped up" in every sense. Scaled up and coloured in intense almost-primaries, they cry out for attention on the flat canvas of this big square shopper. One side is in a zingy circle print while the other is serenely sculptural, using the same print to make sweetie-shaped buttons.

MATERIALS/CUTTING LIST

Plain face fabric
front panel: 34x45cm (13½x18in)
sides: 2 pieces 13x39cm (5x15½in)

Patterned face fabric
back panel: 34x44.5cm (13x18in)

Lining fabric
front and back: 2 pieces 34x45cm
(13½x18in)
sides: 2 pieces 13x39cm (5x15½in)

Heavyweight buckram or plastic canvas
2 pieces 30x35cm (12x14in)

Sewing thread to match face fabric

Fusible hemming web

Curved needle

Water-soluble fabric marker pen

Button forms to cover
12 at 29mm (1⅛in) diam.

MARKING THE HANDLE HOLES

Cut a 13x5cm (5x2in) rectangular hole centrally and 6cm (2¼in) down from the top edge of both pieces of buckram. Use one of these as a template to mark the handle holes onto the reverse of both face fabrics and the lining **(A)**.

A Mark out the handle holes onto the face fabric using the buckram template.

CUTTING THE HANDLE HOLES

On each piece of face and lining fabric, staystitch around the handle holes. Cut an x-shaped slit towards the corners of each handle hole **(B)**.

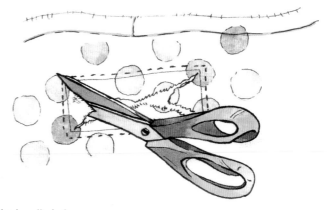

B Cut the handle holes back to the staystitching.

Place the buttons with geometric precision for Modernist cool.

The boxy, stiffened shape protects contents such as library books or magazines that need to remain flat.

Cover the buttons with different coloured fabrics of your choice.

ASSEMBLING THE MAIN BAG

Machine stitch for 2cm (¾in) along each side seam, 4cm (1½in) up from the bottom seam, on the front, back, and side panels. Pin, baste, and stitch the side seams of the front, back, and side panels together, right sides facing **(C)**. Pin, baste, and stitch the bottom edges of the front and back panels together. Clip into the seam allowance at the corners. Turn the bag right side out. Make the lining in the same way, but leave the bottom seam open.

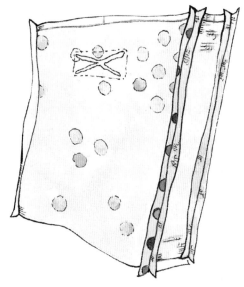

C Join the face fabrics together.

ATTACHING THE LINING

Place the main bag inside the lining, right sides facing, and align the raw edges around the top edge. Pin, baste, and stitch them together. Press the seam toward the lining.

INSERTING THE BUCKRAM

Place the buckram in the bag, trapping its edges within the seam allowance of the face fabric. Secure it to the seam allowance at the sides and bottom corners using strips of fusible hemming web. Slipstitch the lining closed, turn it into the main bag, and secure it to the bottom corners with a few hand stitches.

TOPSTITCHING THE BAG

Topstitch around the top of the bag 3mm (⅛in) down from the edge **(D)**.

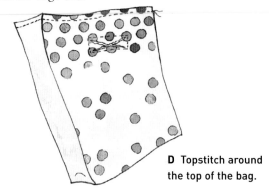

D Topstitch around the top of the bag.

ADDING THE BUTTONS

Using a water-soluble pen, mark out the positions of the buttons on the plain side of the bag. Cut 12 circles of fabric to cover the button forms, sized according to the manufacturer's directions. Ease a fabric circle over the prongs on each button form **(E)**. Secure the metal button-back. Cover 12 buttons and stitch them in place on the bag.

E Cover the buttons with fabric.

FINISHING OFF

Using a curved needle, slipstitch the face fabric to the lining around the handle holes **(F)**.

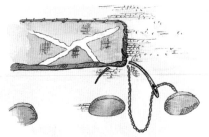

F Slipstich around the handle holes.

Two bags for the price of one – coolly detached dots on cream on one side, a polka-dot party running riot on the other.

Miracle Whip Scarf Bag

This useful bag folds down to almost nothing, to slip into a pocket or desk drawer. It's perfect for lunchtime shopping trips, to save the ubiquitous plastic carrier bag revealing its contents to all.

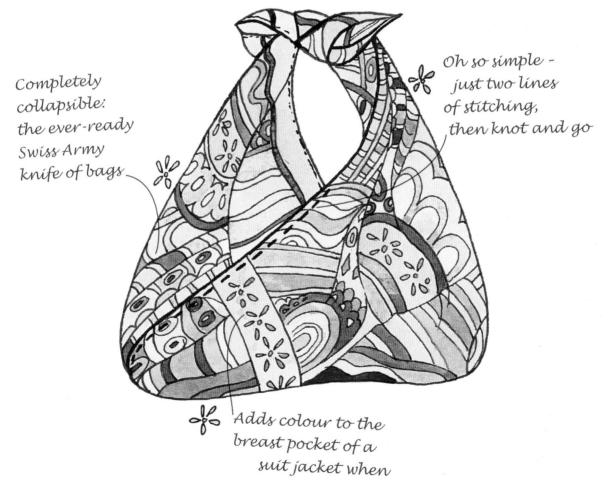

Completely collapsible: the ever-ready Swiss Army knife of bags

Oh so simple – just two lines of stitching, then knot and go

Adds colour to the breast pocket of a suit jacket when not in use as a bag

Miracle Whip Scarf Bag

A photographer I once worked with in my job as a stylist said I had an unusually overdeveloped talent for arranging folded fabric. That's an odd compliment, and perhaps an even odder skill. Since then I noticed that I do indeed absent-mindedly fold and arrange any textiles that come my way – scarves, blankets, towels, even dishcloths! I fiddle with fabric the way some people play with their hair, or peel the labels from beer bottles. Borderline obsessive compulsive behaviour does have its rewards though. The result of one such fiddling session was this cunning little creation, which fits in a pocket yet shakes out to be a thoroughly useful little bag.

MATERIALS/CUTTING LIST

Silky scarf or fabric 20x60cm (8x24in), or any size of the same proportions (hem around all the edges if you are using unhemmed fabric)
Sewing thread to match scarf

FOLDING THE SCARF

Mark out the scarf into equal thirds. Fold one third of the scarf over from one fold line to the other, right sides facing. Stitch together close to one of the edges to secure the fold. Fold the free corner back to the first fold line **(A)**.

A Stitch the first seam.

FINISHING THE BAG

Fold the remaining third of the scarf along its fold line. Stitch to form the opposite seam, close to the edge **(B)**. Turn the bag right side out. Tie the two loose corners together and … hey presto!

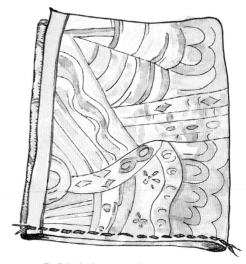

B Stitch the second seam.

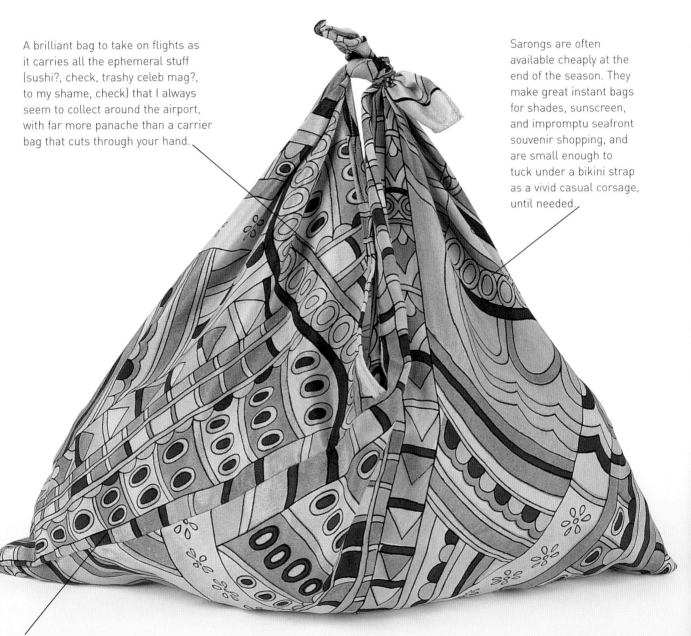

A brilliant bag to take on flights as it carries all the ephemeral stuff (sushi?, check, trashy celeb mag?, to my shame, check) that I always seem to collect around the airport, with far more panache than a carrier bag that cuts through your hand.

Sarongs are often available cheaply at the end of the season. They make great instant bags for shades, sunscreen, and impromptu seafront souvenir shopping, and are small enough to tuck under a bikini strap as a vivid casual corsage, until needed.

Choose a bright but forgiving pattern in a springy, non-creasing synthetic fabric, so that your bag emerges looking like a superslick hot-to-trot butterfly from its folded chrysalis, not a limp rag.

Frilly Frou-Frou Bag

Not quite an explosion in a haberdashery store, but almost - this bag joyously mixes every sort of trim on riotous, polka-dot stripes.

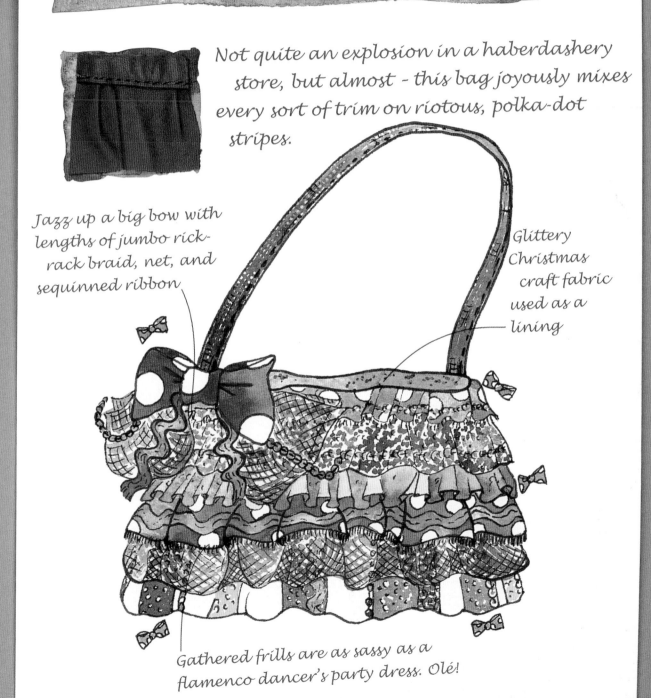

Jazz up a big bow with lengths of jumbo rick-rack braid, net, and sequinned ribbon

Glittery Christmas craft fabric used as a lining

Gathered frills are as sassy as a flamenco dancer's party dress. Olé!

Frilly Frou-Frou Bag

Polka dots and frills are a killer combination, culminating in the flirty ra-ra skirts and oversized bows popularized by unlikely trendsetter Minnie Mouse, and revisited in the '80s by canny fashionista Madonna at the peak of her cutesie-pie powers. How to wear today? Teens and early twenties can pull all of their toys out of the dressing up box and go to town with trashy mismatched plastic bangles and overscaled button earrings. Older gals in lurve with cheap frills need to add a dash more irony by playing the outfit down and letting this bag do the shouting. Now boogie!

MATERIALS/CUTTING LIST

Dark denim fabric
main bag: 2 pieces 33x18cm (13x7in)
handle: 68x9cm (27x3½in)
Red glittery cotton lining fabric 2 pieces
33x18cm (13x7in)
Firm iron-on interfacing 4 pieces 33x18cm
(13x7in); 1 piece 68x9cm (27x3½in)
Pink polka-dot fabric cut with selvedge
on lower long edge: 40x5cm (16x2in)
Green metallic braid
40cm (16in) x 3mm (⅛in) wide
Sewing thread to match fabrics and trims
Black polka-dot fabric cut with selvedge
on lower long edge: 45x7.5cm (18x3in)
Multicoloured sequin ribbon 45cm (18in)
Burnt orange suede 5x50cm (2x20in)
Red polka-dot fabric cut with selvedge
on lower long edge: 10x55cm (4x22in)
Blue satiny rick-rack braid 56x1cm (22x⅜in)
Pink netting 15x66cm (6x26in)
Striped polka-dot fabric 25x66cm (10x26in)
**Assorted rick-rack braid, cotton lace,
beading, sequins** in 15cm (6in) lengths
Sewing thread in red
Red-and-white polka-dot fabric for the
bow: 30x15cm (12x6in) and 7.5x9cm (3x3½in)
Red net 20x35cm (8x14in)
Wide blue rick-rack braid 25cm (10in) long
Green sequin ribbon 25cm (10in) long
SEE PAGE 125 FOR TEMPLATE
Enlarge template to 196%,
using a photocopier as necessary.

PREPARING THE FABRIC

Apply iron-on interfacing to the wrong side of the lining and face fabrics for the main bag and handle. Using the template, mark and cut out the pattern as directed.

DECORATING THE FABRIC

Pin, baste, and stitch the green metallic braid 7.5mm (¼in) up from the selvedge of the pink polka-dot fabric. Turn the top raw edge under twice and work a gathering stitch to gather it until it fits the top edge of the bag front. Pin, baste, and stitch the frill in place just inside the seam allowance at the top edge of the bag front. Make three more frills, using black polka-dot fabric with sequin ribbon, then suede, followed by red polka-dot fabric with blue rick-rack, attaching them along the next three marked stitch lines **(A)**.

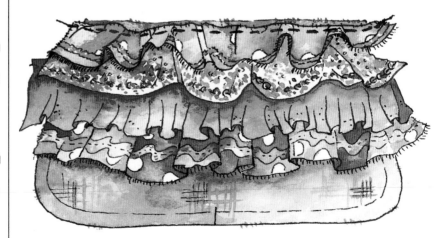

A Attach the frills to the bag front.

Dark denim is variously soooo over and soooo now. Ignore fashion's vagaries and make up your own mind. With this combo of colours and patterns you know dark denim makes sense.

Sassy red topstitching gives "glamour-girl go-faster-stripe" edginess to the slick, pencil-slim handle.

There's something ineffably cheeky yet innocent about rick-rack braid. Vary the widths and colours for a hint of naughty schoolgirl charm.

Using selvedges deliberately at the lower edges of the frills scores high in two departments. It saves hemming and also adds a choppy, roughed-up vibe that lifts the look out of full-on '80s puffball remix hell.

PREPARING THE PINK NETTING

Fold the pink netting in half lengthwise and stitch the long edges together. Trim the seam allowance to 7.5mm (⅛in) and turn the tube right side out. Gather the net along the seamed edge and pull it up until it fits across the bag front along the next marked stitch line **(B)**.

B Gather the tube of net along the seam.

ATTACHING THE BOTTOM FRILL

Fold the striped polka-dot fabric in half lengthwise, right sides facing, and stitch the long edges together. Turn the tube right side out. Decorate the fabric as desired with rick-rack braid, cotton lace, beading, and sequins. Gather the frill along the seamed edge and pull it up until it fits across the bag front. Stitch it in place along the bottom marked line **(C)**.

C Stitch on the final frill.

ATTACHING THE PINK FRILL

Pin, baste, and stitch the pink net frill in place along the remaining marked line, above the striped polka-dot frill.

FINISHING THE FRILLS

Pin and baste the lower edge of the bottom frill clear of the seam allowance. Pin and baste the raw side edges of each frill in place just inside the seam allowance **(D)**. Arrange the frills towards the body of the bag so that the frill will have sufficient volume to puff out appealingly when the bag is turned right side out.

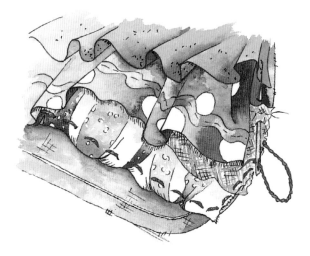

D Baste the frills ready for assembling the bag.

MAKING THE HANDLE

Fold the handle fabric in half lengthwise, wrong sides facing. Pin, baste, and stitch the long edges together. Trim the seam allowance to 3mm (⅛in). Fold the handle in half lengthwise, concealing the seam allowance. Topstitch the long edges together using red thread **(E)**.

E Topstitch the handle in contrasting thread.

ASSEMBLING THE BAG

Follow the instructions for making a basic lined tote bag (*see* p.118), positioning one end of the handle at the left-hand corner of the front of the bag and the other end at the left-hand corner on the back of the bag. Trim the seam allowances to 7.5mm (¼in) and clip into the seam allowances around the curves. Stitch around the edge of the bag **(F)**.

F Stitch around the edges of the bag.

MAKING THE BOW

Fold the larger piece of fabric for the bow in half lengthwise, right sides facing. Pin, baste, and stitch the long edges together. Trim the seam allowance and turn the fabric right side out. Press the fabric so that the seam is along the centre back. Fold each short end towards the middle and tuck one into the other. Turn under the raw edge and slipstitch the ends together. Fold the smaller piece of fabric in half lengthwise, right sides facing. Stitch the long edges together. Trim the seam allowance and turn the fabric right side out. Wrap this piece of fabric around the centre of the bow. Tuck in the raw edges and stitch them together **(G)**.

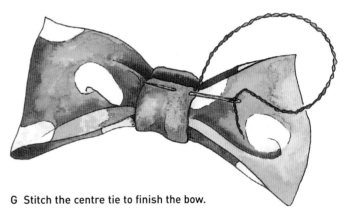

G Stitch the centre tie to finish the bow.

DECORATING THE BOW

Feed the net, sequin ribbon, and rick-rack braid through the base of the bow tie. Secure them in place with a few stitches. Stitch the bow in place just in front of the handle on the front of the bag.

Can't Knit, Won't Knit Bag

Let someone else do the knitting!
A ready-made sweater, decorated with
ribbons, sequins, and a knitted corsage,
is all you need to create this darling
little bag in a teensy amount of time.

Embellish with
store-bought
corsages or hair
ornaments

Gaily coloured
fabric makes a
suitably peppy lining

1940s-style
Fair Isle sweater
gets a new
lease of life

Decorate a
plain sweater with
sequins or beads

Add pizazz with
velvet ribbon
secured with
sequins

Can't Knit, Won't Knit Bag

Knitting is a craft I haven't yet got around to mastering, which is probably why I drool about all things knitted. The soft, squooshy appeal of a sweater makes it a deliciously tempting starting point for a new handbag. End-of-season sales are a great hunting ground for pristine knitted bargains, while thrift shops and jumble sales yield vintage Fair Isle tank tops just crying out for reincarnation as funky bags. If moths have nibbled at your favourite sweater, simply stitch the hole closed and cover the damage with ribbon and sequins!

MATERIALS/CUTTING LIST

Knitted sweater
front and back: 2 pieces 25x30cm (10x12in)
handles: 2 pieces 40x10cm (16x4in)
Assorted sequins and ribbon
Sewing thread to match sweater, sequins, and ribbon
Cord: 2 lengths
50cm (20in) x 6mm (¼in) wide
Large safety pin
Lining fabric 2 pieces 25x30cm (10x12in)
Purchased knitted corsage

CREATING THE FACE FABRIC

Decorate the front panel as desired, attaching sequins and ribbon **(A)**.

MAKING THE HANDLES

Fold a piece of the handle fabric around a length of cord, right sides facing. Pin, baste, and stitch close to the cord **(B)**. Remove the cord and trim the seam allowance to 7.5mm (¼in). Turn the handle right side out. Attach the safety pin to the end of the cord and feed this end of the cord through the handle. Make a second handle in the same way.

A Decorate the face fabric with ribbon and sequins.

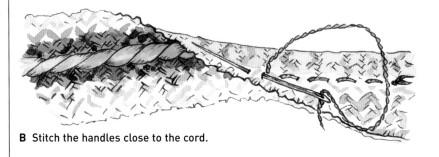

B Stitch the handles close to the cord.

ASSEMBLING AND FINISHING THE BAG

Make up the bag following the instructions for a basic lined tote bag (*see* p.118). Turn the bag right side out, close the lining, and attach the knitted corsage.

Cord-filled handles are strong and retain their perky shape.

A gloriously scrunchy detachable knitted corsage adds a kind of adorable "little-orphan-Annie" appeal, which suits the nostalgic vibe.

A sale-rail sweater gives a quick result that looks like a beautifully hand-crafted labour of love.

Stitch on as many or as few sequins and beads as you like – it's your bag.

Urban Scrapbook Bag

Celebrate the flotsam and jetsam of a life well lived in this appealingly tactile little number, which can be added to endlessly as you collect new pieces and fresh memories.

Photocopy a map onto fabric, mark key sites with an embroidered cross, and scrunch fabric before stitching on

Baubles, beads, and bracelets add hippy chic

Emblem from an old college jacket or blazer badge

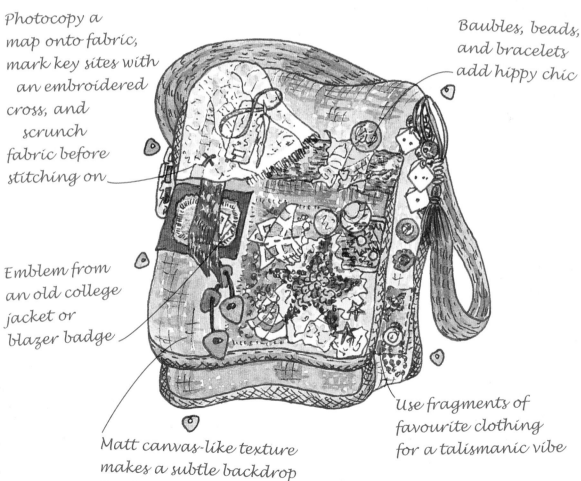

Use fragments of favourite clothing for a talismanic vibe

Matt canvas-like texture makes a subtle backdrop for diverse materials

Urban Scrapbook Bag

I'm a massive fan of scrapbooking. What I want, though, is not sterile, punched-plastic sleeves, but the take-me-there treat of rough sugar paper, crumbling beneath the weight of layered ephemera. This bag, which can be customized for boys or girls, is a groovy journal of good times, with plenty of space to record those still to come.

MATERIALS/CUTTING LIST

Paper ephemera e.g. tickets, flyers, sweet wrappers, maps, doodles, love notes, and photographs

Coloured crayons or pens

Badge-making kit and/or ready-made badges

Paper adhesive

White cotton fabric e.g. an old pillowcase

Guitar picks

Eyelet kit

Leather thonging

Button forms to cover

Army surplus-type bag

Fabric adhesive

New and recycled haberdashery e.g. sequinned and embroidered patches and brocade ribbons

Assorted patches and scraps e.g. from a college jacket, guitar strap, or favourite pair of jeans

Sewing thread to match ephemera

Embroidery thread in assorted shades

Buttons, charms, beads, keyrings, and old jewellery

Faux rhinestones

YOU WILL NEED ACCESS TO A PHOTOCOPIER, AND LATER TO A COPY SHOP FOR COPYING TO FABRIC

PREPARING THE DECORATION

Photocopy the paper ephemera you wish to colour. Colour the copies using crayons or pens. Photocopy other favourite paper ephemera and make them into badges with the badge-making kit, following the manufacturer's directions **(A)**.

A Colour a paper photocopy before transferring the image to the fabric.

MAKING FABRIC TRANSFERS

Arrange the items you want to transfer to fabric onto an A4 sheet of paper, as if compiling a scrapbook page. Leave space around some items and overlap others. Glue them in place. Take your design to a copy shop and have it printed onto the white fabric.

PREPARING MORE EPHEMERA

Prepare any other items you want to attach to the bag. Following the eyelet manufacturer's directions, punch holes in guitar picks and affix the eyelets, then thread the picks onto leather thonging, knotting between each one. Cover button forms with some of the photocopied fabric.

ATTACHING THE DECORATION

Cut around the photocopied fabric shapes. Pin layers of fabric ephemera on the front and sides of the bag until you are happy with the design **(B)**. Crumple and fold some items for a lively, windblown effect. Stitch the items in place and highlight some areas with simple stitches. Sew on the buttons and charms, and glue on the rhinestones.

B Check you are happy with the design before stitching.

Scraps of treasured guitar strap keep you in touch with your inner rock god, or goddess.

Laminate cherished paper ephemera to create different textures.

Handmade badges transform doodles into wearable works of art.

No self-respecting rock star leaves home without at least a little sparkle. Forget bling – gold is so, well, obvious. Rhinestones and sequins in muted moss and earth shades whisper, rather than scream, star quality.

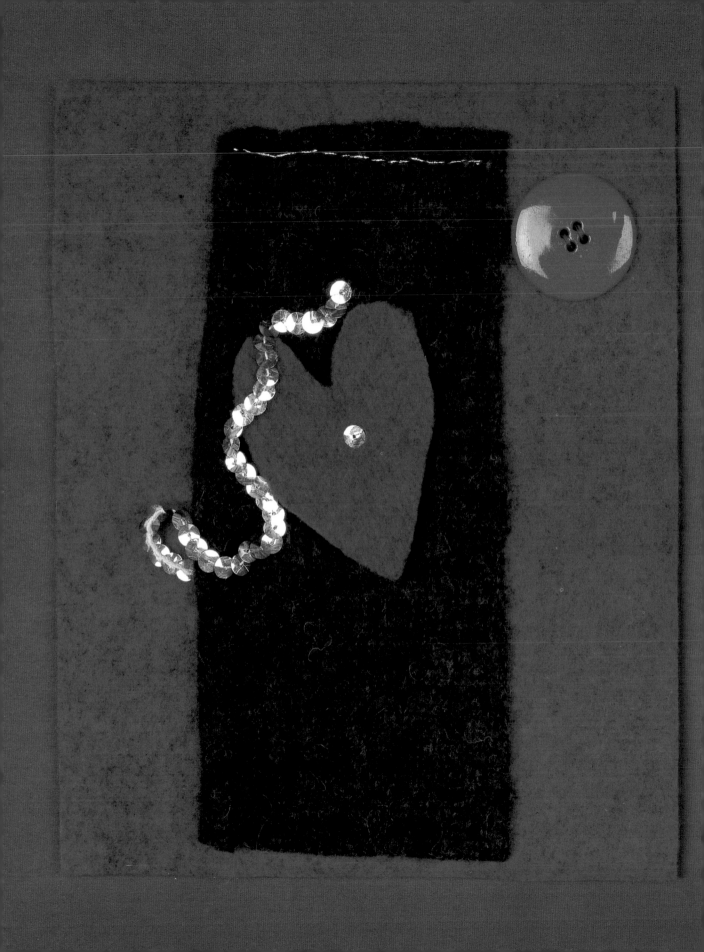

Heart Motif Felt Bag

Felt comes out of the craft cupboard and onto the catwalk with this cool combo of burgundy, grape, and cherry.

Overscaled buttons add drama and panache

Randomly sized buttons give a quirky, fun look; stick to one colour to unify motifs

Warm deep-pile felted wool is as cosy and welcoming as an après-ski hot chocolate

Metallic machine-stitching illuminates dark-toned felt and adds definition

Heart Motif Felt Bag

Felt is a delightful medium for creative stitching. It lends itself perfectly to appliqué as the edges do not unravel and it clings to itself, making it blissfully easy to plan and rearrange your design. As well as being practical, felt has a glorious tactile scrumptiousness and is available in an endless array of colours. Forget those paintbox primaries of mean, thin squares dimly remembered from school craft sessions. This is felt used as a rich, comforting, luxurious fabric. The result is highly strokeable, so prepare to make new friends, keen to get up close and personal with your handbag!

MATERIALS/CUTTING LIST

Felted knitted fabric purchased or made by washing woollen knits on a very hot wash and tumble drying for extra felting
bag: 35x70cm (14x28in)
contrast border: 70x12cm (28x4¾in)
handles: 2 pieces 86x12cm (34x4¾in)
Felt in toning shades for front pocket: 4x6cm (1½x2¼in); 4x2.5cm (1½x1in)
Felt in toning shades for back pocket: 13x12cm (5x4¾in); 13x6cm (5x2¼in); 7x9cm (2¾x3½in) for a heart shape
Felt in toning shades for motifs: 8x11cm (3¼x4¼in); 9x10cm (3½x4in); 8x8cm (3¼x3¼in)
Felt in toning shades for heart shapes: 9 pieces 5x9cm (2x3½in)
Sewing thread to match felts
Metallic machine sewing thread
Sequins
Buttons in toning colours and various sizes
Large matching buttons 4

NOTE: Use a large machine zigzag or stretch stitch throughout unless the directions state otherwise.

MEASURING AND CUTTING OUT

Mark and cut out all the pattern pieces. Draw and cut out nine heart shapes, including four single ones and three paired shapes of slightly different sizes to make layered hearts.

MAKING THE BACK POCKET

Pin the smaller piece of felt for the back pocket on top of the larger piece, aligning the top edges. Stitch them together along the top and bottom edges of the top piece of felt, leaving the side edges unstitched. Pin, baste, and stitch the heart motif centrally on this pieced felt **(A)**.

A Assemble the back pocket.

MAKING THE FRONT POCKET

Pin and baste the smaller piece of felt for the front pocket centrally halfway down the larger piece. Stitch down the long edges of the top strip, leaving the side edges unstitched. Stitch close along the top edge of the pocket to give it extra stability.

Sequins add sparkle and glitz. Use them sparingly to keep the look sophisticated, or go overboard for a hint of Vegas.

Using different but toning colours within the same palette adds interest but keeps the design sleek, rather than childlike.

Use alternative motifs if hearts don't appeal, but keep the shapes simple and not too intricate.

This tiny pocket will keep your travel ticket to hand.

Organic, curvy shapes work best with the sort of folksy, variable edge that tends to develop naturally as you stitch.

ATTACHING THE BACK POCKET

Fold the main panel for the bag in half widthwise. Pin and baste the large pocket centrally on the back of the bag, with the top edge of the pocket 9cm (3½in) down from the top edge of the back of the bag. Stitch the pocket in place around its side and bottom edges, leaving the top edge open.

DECORATING THE FRONT OF THE BAG

Fold the main panel for the bag in half widthwise to find the centre line down the front. Centre the felt for the top middle square at a slight angle on the line, 6cm (2¼in) down from the top edge of the front of the bag. Pin, baste, and stitch the square in place. Stitch the appropriate heart shape on top. Pin, baste, and stitch the other motifs across the front panel, evenly spaced, and layer the pieces in a similar way. Using metallic thread, and with the machine set to a long straight stitch, work decorative stitching around and over the motifs, as desired. Stitch sequins and buttons in place **(B)**.

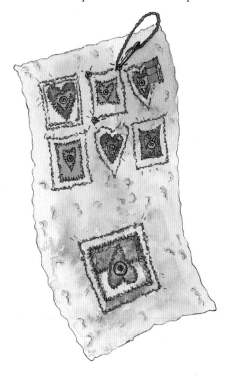

B Add the sequins, buttons, and metallic thread.

ATTACHING THE FRONT POCKET

Pin, baste, and stitch the pocket onto the top right-hand corner of the bag front, overlapping the hearts beneath. Stitch around three of the edges, leaving the top edge open.

ASSEMBLING THE BAG

Pin, baste, and stitch the side seams of the front and back panels together, right sides facing. Cut out a 2cm (¾in) square at each bottom corner of the bag **(C)**.

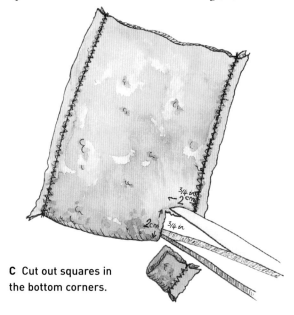

C Cut out squares in the bottom corners.

STITCHING THE GUSSET

Open out each corner and align the newly cut edges. Pin, baste, and stitch the gusset seam **(D)**. Steam iron through a cloth to press the felt flat. Turn the bag right side out.

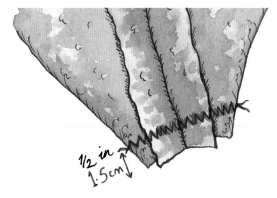

D Stitch across the bottom corners.

MAKING THE HANDLES

Fold each strip of felt for the handles into three, lengthwise. Pin, baste, and stitch each strip down the centre line (E).

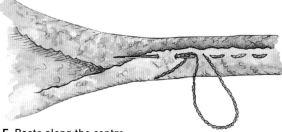

E Baste along the centre of each handle.

ATTACHING THE HANDLES

Pin and baste the handles on the front and back panels, positioning each end 11.5cm (4½in) in from the nearest side seam, with the raw ends protruding 2cm (¾in) above the top edge of the bag.

ATTACHING THE CUFF

Stitch the two short ends of the cuff together. Fold the cuff in half lengthwise. Slip the cuff over the top edge of the bag, right sides facing, aligning the raw edges and positioning the seam in the cuff centrally on the back of the bag. Pin, baste, and stitch both layers of the cuff to the top edge of the bag (F).

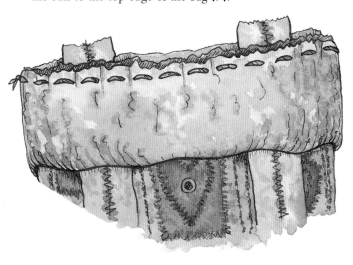

F Baste the cuff to the top of the bag.

FINISHING THE HANDLES

Trim the ends of the handles flush with the top edge of the bag. Turn up the cuff and the handles. Stitch across the bottom ends of each handle, 3mm (⅛in) down from the top edge, to secure them to the cuff (G). Stitch a large button in place at the base of each end of each handle.

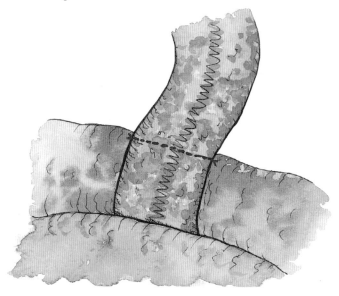

G Stitch the handle to the top of the cuff to secure in place.

Leabharlanna Fhine Gall

Beaded Floral Bag

This is the perfect bag for a summer's afternoon or evening. It also provides a great pep-up to transform daywear into after-work special occasion material. The detachable organza floral corsage creates a "nouveau nostalgia" vibe.

Wired crystal beads from a gift-wrapped soap reveal a welcome use for scraps

Single broad handle balances the shape of the bag

Boldly patterned fabric withstands and guides decoration with beads, sequins, and decorative stitches

Grosgrain ribbon adds crispness to the upper edge

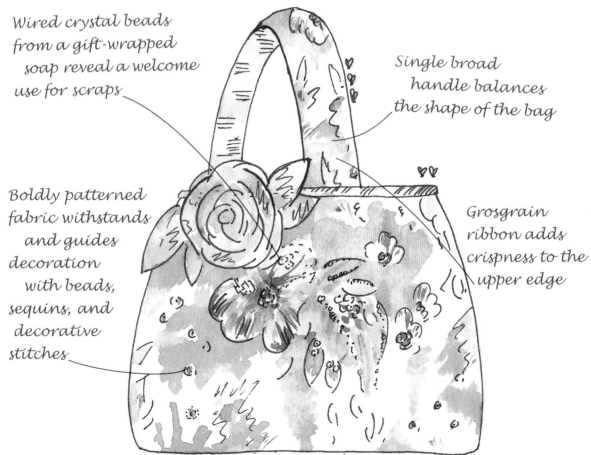

Beaded Floral Bag

I suffered a huge crisis of confidence designing this bag. The fabric jumped out at me and forced me to buy it as the store was closing, but for days I suffered a nagging fear that perhaps I had gone just a little bit too far down a "Liberace-goes-to-Hawaii" route in my choice. However, as I stitched into it, the fabric's audacious alchemy of colour and pattern got my textile mojo working, and I found that the more embroidery and beading I threw at the bag, the better it looked. Different textures of thread, beads, and sequins were all just mopped up and rendered coherent by that luscious patterning, and even the corsage cried out for showgirl glitz and sparkle.

MATERIALS/CUTTING LIST

Face fabric
front and back: 2 pieces 30x30cm (12x12in)
handle: 4.5x45cm (1¾x18in)
Lining 2 pieces 30x30cm (12x12in)
Firm iron-on interfacing 4 pieces 30x30cm
(12x12in); 1 piece 4.5x45cm (1¾x18in)
Grosgrain ribbon
to decorate top edge of main bag: 2 pieces
35cm (14in) by 4.5cm (1¾in) wide
handle lining: 4.5x45cm (1¾x18in)
Sewing thread to match face fabric, lining,
bias binding, and corsage
Beading needle
Silk thread for beading
Assorted tiny beads and sequins
Assorted embroidery threads
Bias binding 2 colours 45cm (18in) length
Organza ribbon 2 colours
1m (40in) x 5cm (2in) wide
Brooch finding
Scraps of green felt
Wired bead stems from florist
or haberdashery department
Small haberdashery flowers
SEE PAGE 125 FOR TEMPLATE
Enlarge template to 244%,
using a photocopier as necessary

PREPARING THE FABRIC

Cut out all the pattern pieces in the face fabric and lining, using the template for the front and bag as directed. Mark out the seam allowances and centre points. Back all the pieces of lining and face fabric, including the handle, with iron-on interfacing.

ATTACHING THE GROSGRAIN RIBBON

Pin, baste, and stitch the grosgrain ribbon in place across the top of the bag, right sides facing and 2.5cm (1in) down from the top edge **(A)**. Turn the ribbon up to conceal the stitch line and press.

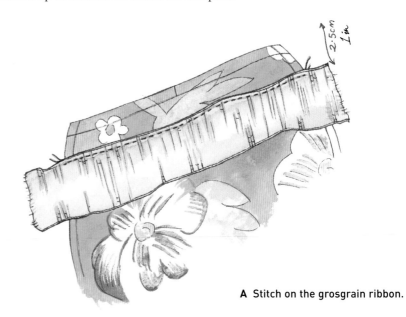

A Stitch on the grosgrain ribbon.

Using the same grosgrain ribbon to edge the bag and back the handle keeps the design flowing. A slightly softer shade than that of the face fabric tones down the look to chi-chi, not beachy.

Use two shades of patterned, rather than plain, organza for the corsage, to give it a 3-D flourish and to keep the look sassy, not matronly.

Choose an intensely patterned piece of the face fabric for the handle, for added interest and to integrate it visually with the body of the bag.

Go wild at the embroidery threads counter. A vivid fabric such as this will soak up as much colour and texture as you can throw at it, and be all the ritzier for its glorious lack of restraint.

DECORATING THE FRONT PANEL

Pick out details of the pattern on the front panel in embroidery, beads, and sequins **(B)**. Try picking out strong lines, such as the veins of leaves or the edges of petals, and highlighting them with a line of beading or filling them with satin stitch (*see* p.121) to add depth and movement. Fill in whole areas, such as petals, with beads, and pick out the centres of flowers or scatter the background with sequins.

B Emphasize the pattern on the fabric with beading, sequins, and embroidery.

ASSEMBLING THE BAG AND LINING

Pin, baste, and stitch the front and back of the bag together along the side and bottom seams, right sides facing **(C)**. Leave the top opening and the bottom corners unstitched. Join the front and back of the lining in the same way, leaving an opening in one side seam for turning at a later stage.

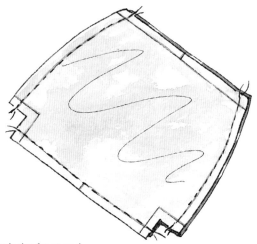

C Stitch the front and back of the bag together.

STITCHING THE GUSSET

Open out one corner of the main bag and align the raw edges. Pin, baste, and stitch this gusset seam **(D)**. Repeat on the other corner. Turn the bag right side out. Stitch the gusset seams on the lining in the same way. Leave the lining wrong side out.

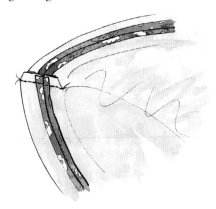

D Stitch across the bottom corner to make a gusset.

MAKING AND ATTACHING THE HANDLE

Decorate the face fabric for the handle with embroidery, beading, and sequins in the same way as for the front of the bag. Pin and baste the face fabric and the grosgrain ribbon together along both long edges, wrong sides facing. Pin and baste a length of bias binding in one colour along one long edge and stitch it in place along the fold mark of the binding. Turn the binding over the raw edge and slipstitch it in place. Attach the binding in the second colour along the other long edge **(E)**.

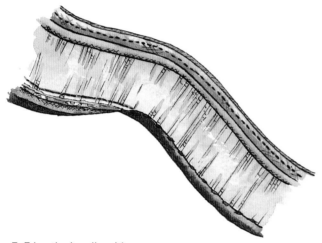

E Edge the handle with two differently coloured bindings.

ASSEMBLING THE BAG

Pin and baste the handle, aligning the raw ends with the top edge of the bag and positioning the centre of each end 5cm (2in) away from the right-hand seam on the front and back panels. Slip the lining over the main bag and handles, right sides facing. Pin, baste, and stitch the lining to the main bag all around the top edge **(F)**. Turn the bag right side out through the opening in the lining and then slipstitch the opening closed.

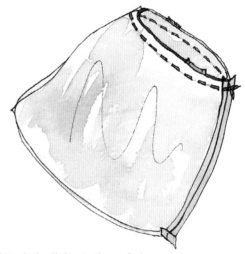

F Attach the lining to the main bag.

MAKING THE ROSE

Place the two organza ribbons one on top of the other. Fold over one end of the ribbons at a 45-degree angle and stitch the end in place (*see* p.32). Roll the ribbons around the folded end to form the centre of the rose and secure it with a stitch. Work a few running stitches along the bottom edge and pull the ribbon into gathers before securing it with another stitch. Continue to gather and secure the ribbon until you have a pleasing shape.

FINISHING THE CORSAGE

Cut simple leaf shapes from the green felt. Stitch the leaves, wired bead stems, haberdashery flowers, and the rose onto the brooch finding. Pin the corsage on the bag.

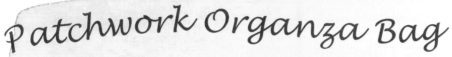

Patchwork Organza Bag

Dainty patchwork bags in hot silk
scraps are embellished with sequins
and metallics for a hint of the East.
Add a ribbon closure and
use as a ditsy little evening bag
for lipstick and keys.

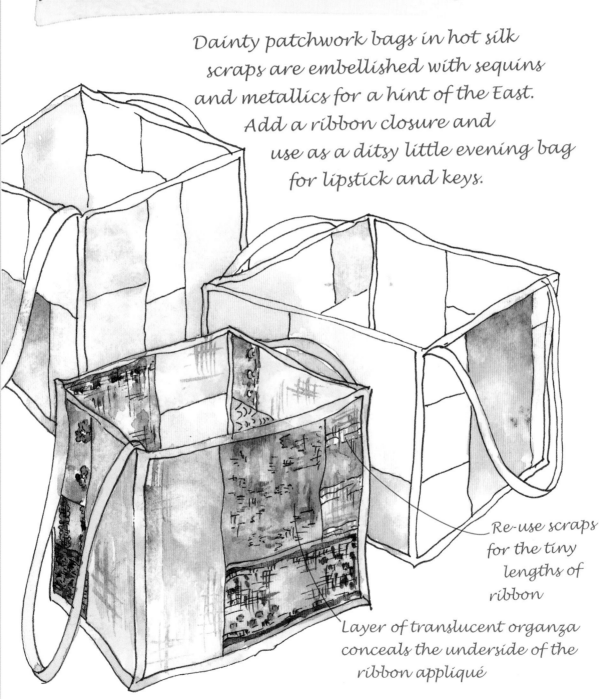

Re-use scraps
for the tiny
lengths of
ribbon

Layer of translucent organza
conceals the underside of the
ribbon appliqué

Patchwork Organza Bags

Haberdashery departments are, to me, the new sweetshops, with the considerable bonus of their stock being calorie-free. I buy ribbon the way normal people buy shoes. These ditsy little bags used up some of my favourite scraps, easing those shopaholic guilt pangs in the prettiest way imaginable. Most shops sell ribbon in lengths as short as 10cm (4in), so you can have a real pick-and-mix splurge without worrying about either the cost or the damage to your waistline.

MATERIALS/CUTTING LIST

Tissue paper

PINK AND GREEN BAGS

Silk fabric see the note below

front and back: 2 pieces 12x13cm (4¾x5in)

sides: 2 pieces 10x13cm (4x5in)

base: 12x10cm (4¾x4in)

Organza

front and back: 2 pieces 12x15 cm (4¾x6in)

sides: 2 pieces 10x15cm (4x6in)

Sheer ribbon for handle: 2 x 38cm (15in)

lengths x 12mm (½in) wide

BLUE BAG

Silk fabric see the note below

front and back: 2 pieces 10x11.5cm (4x4½in)

sides: 2 pieces 8x11.5cm (3¼x4½in)

base: 10x8cm (4x3¼in)

Organza

front and back: 2 pieces 10x11.5cm (4x4½in)

sides: 2 pieces 8x11.5cm (3¼x4½in)

Sheer ribbon for handle: 2 x 30cm (12in)

lengths x 12mm (½in) wide

Thread to tone with organza, silk, and ribbons

Assorted lengths ribbons up to 11cm (4¼in)

Beading needle

Assorted tiny beads

Assorted sequins

Note: A 1cm (⅜in) seam allowance is used throughout. Position the top edge of each silk panel along the selvedge.

CREATING THE FACE FABRIC

Draw out the face dimensions for the front of the bag onto tissue paper, and mark out a 1cm (⅜in) seam allowances. Pin and baste the paper to the wrong side of the organza. Pin the ribbons in blocks onto the organza; make sure they are clear of the seam allowance and tuck under visible raw ends. When you are happy with the design, baste and stitch the ribbons in place **(A)**. Add beads and sequins as desired. Carefully tear away the tissue paper. Repeat the process for the other panels.

A Baste and stitch the ribbons onto the organza.

Frayed edges give a flamboyant, gypsyish flair, which breaks up the geometry into something enticingly bohemian.

Metallic ribbons glint quietly from the depths of moody, inky backgrounds.

Flirty, flippy organza ribbons dance about these delicious little bags like butterfly wings, yet are strong enough to be practical.

Shot silk in jewel shades adds a hint of "Arabian Night" to the dullest day.

ASSEMBLING THE BAG

Pin and baste each panel of organza to the corresponding silk panel, so that the organza protrudes above the silk along the top edges. Pin, baste, and stitch the sides of the bag together, right sides facing. Then pin, baste, and stitch the base in place **(B)**.

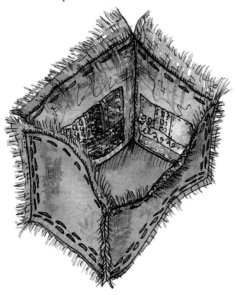

B Baste the panels and base of the bag together.

TOPSTITCHING THE BAG

Turn the bag right side out and trim the seam allowance to 4mm (³⁄₁₆in). Topstitch along each side seam and around the base, 4mm (³⁄₁₆in) in from the edge **(C)**. Leave the top edge unstitched.

C Topstitch along the side seams.

ATTACHING THE HANDLES

Fold back 4cm (1½in) at each end of one length of sheer organza ribbon. Baste each fold in position, 1.5cm (½in) down from the top edge on the front of the bag to form the first handle. Repeat to attach the second handle. Fold down the top selvedge of the bag over the ribbon. Topstitch around the edge 4mm (³⁄₁₆in) down from the edge **(D)**.

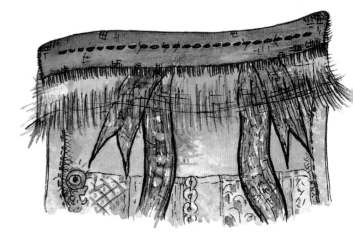

D Topstitch around the top edge of the bag.

ADAPTING THE DESIGN

To make even more of a feature of the organza, you could sew the panels for the bag together with wrong sides facing. Then fray each seam allowance back almost to the stitch line. Do not topstitch along the seams, only around the top edge to secure the handles.

Techniques

GENERAL NOTES AND METHODS

All measurements are given width first, height second. This is especially important when using pictorial fabrics so that the image will be the right way up on the finished bag. Use either metric or imperial measurements; do not combine the two, as inaccuracies in fit might occur.

Unless stated otherwise, a seam allowance of 1.5cm (⅝in) is used throughout, and all seams are pressed open. Assuming the fabrics are suitable for pressing, begin by pressing and then press at each stage of the work for a professional-looking finish. Press through a muslin cloth to protect the fabric.

Unless stated otherwise, back all the face and lining fabrics with firm iron-on interfacing (following the manufacturer's directions) before marking and cutting out the pattern. This adds stability to the fabrics and gives the finished bag greater strength. It also eases cutting out and making up, especially with slippery fabrics like satin. You can dramatically alter the feel and look of a bag by using a lighter weight of interfacing, or omitting it entirely.

Remove all pins as soon as basting (tacking) is done, and basting threads when the finished stitching is complete. This aids pressing and ensures pins are not left in the finished bag.

BASIC EQUIPMENT

Assemble a basic sewing kit, sufficient for making any of the bag designs. More specialist tools are listed for specific projects, but the items below will be useful throughout:

Dressmaking shears: essential for cutting fabric accurately.
Embroidery scissors: useful for trimming thread ends without slashing the fabric, and for removing basting stitches.
Floristry scissors: with tough notches for gripping and clipping the wire in wire-edged ribbon.
Paper scissors: medium-sized for cutting templates.
Iron, ironing cloth, and ironing board or mat: use a damp piece of muslin to protect fabric.
Glass-headed pins: easy to see and comfortable to use; especially good for pinning through multiple layers.

Fine dressmaking pins: to avoid marking delicate fabrics.
Flat-headed quilting pins: useful when working with thick fabrics, such as felted wool.
Sharps needles: for general hand-stitching; strong, with a short, round eye. Sizes 8 or 9 are useful, multi-purpose sizes.
Beading needles: very useful for beading work as they are fine and flexible enough to pick up several beads at a time.
Machine needles: size 90 (14) needles are a good all-round choice; change them frequently for the best results.
HB pencil and sharpener
Sewing machine (but all projects can be hand-sewn)
Tape measure
Set square and ruler: for marking-out geometric shapes.
Tracing paper or greaseproof paper (an inexpensive alternative that comes on a roll for ecomomical use).
Dressmakers' carbon paper and ballpoint pen: in various colours, an easy way to transfer designs onto fabric.
Water-soluble fabric marker pen: for drawing directly onto fabric without leaving a permanent mark; useful for transferring pattern markings and marking seam lines.

TRANSFERRING PATTERNS

If the pattern is given at the actual size, simply trace it off onto tracing or greaseproof paper, and cut it out. If it needs to be enlarged, photocopy or scale it up to the correct size (percentages are given on each pattern). Unless stated otherwise, place the pattern on the wrong side of the fabric and draw around the outline with a water-soluble pen **(A)**.

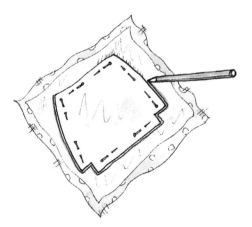

A Draw the outline with a water-soluble fabric marker pen.

Transfer any additional pattern markings using basting (tacking) stitches, or simply push a pin through the paper at any points that need to be marked, and draw these on clearly with the pen. Mark all pattern markings, including the seam allowances, onto the front of the fabrics as well as the reverse to make accurate assembly easier. Mark out the centre marks along each edges of fabric so you can match the pieces accurately when assembling the bag. The water-soluble pen marks can be sponged away later. If marking on very dark fabric, use tailors' chalk or dressmakers' pencil in a pale shade.

MAKING A BASIC LINED TOTE BAG

Prepare the lining and face fabrics by backing them with fusible interfacing. Mark out the front and back panels in both lining and face fabrics. Using a water-soluble pen, mark on the seam allowances and centres, and cut out the panels. Place the panels of face fabric together, right sides facing. Pin, baste, and stitch around the sides and lower edge. Turn right side out. Repeat for the lining, with an opening along one side for turning. Leave the lining wrong side out.

Make the handles by the method given for a specific design, or by folding a length of fabric in half lengthwise, right sides together. Baste and stitch the long edges and turn right side out. Pin and baste the handles in place on the right side of the bag, so that the handle ends protrude slightly above the top raw edges of the bag. Reinforce the handles by stitching across them just inside the seam allowance.

Put the main bag inside the lining, right sides facing (A). Pin, baste, and stitch the bag and lining together around the top edge, matching the centres and side seams. Trim away any excess from the raw ends of the handles.

A Put the main bag inside the lining.

Turn the bag right side out through the opening in the lining. Slipstitch the opening closed (B).

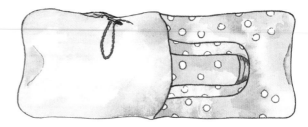

B Slipstitch the opening in the lining closed.

MAKING AND APPLYING BIAS BINDING

Unless the pattern states otherwise, mark and cut out 3cm-wide (¼in) strips across the bias of the fabric (A). Fold in each long edge towards the centre line on the wrong side and press.

A Mark and cut out strips on the bias.

There are two ways of applying bias binding. For the method used on the Baby Change Bag (see pp.52–7), simply fold the binding around the edges of the bag and then pin, baste, and machine it in place. This produces a strong result and gives a crisp, topstitched look. Where you do not want a visible line of stitching, as on the handle of the Beaded Floral Bag (see pp.106–11), use the traditional method of applying binding. Pin, baste, and machine stitch one side of the binding along the edge of the handle, right sides facing with raw edges aligned. Fold the binding over the raw edge and slipstitch it in place.

EMBELLISHING WITH DECORATION
Attaching single beads

Bring the needle up to the front of the fabric. Pick up a bead on the tip of the needle and slide it onto the thread. Push the needle back down through the fabric, matching the length of stitch to the length of the bead, so that the bead sits neatly and securely in place **(A)**. If the stitch is too short the bead will not sit smoothly and will distort the surface of the fabric; if the stitch is too long, the work will look unsightly and the bead will move around.

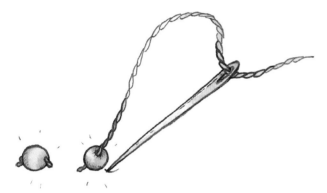

A Match the length of the stitch to the length of the bead

Attaching single sequins

Bring the needle to the front of the fabric and up through the hole in the sequin. Make a short stitch horizontally across the sequin to the right, passing back down through the fabric. Return the needle up through the hole in the sequin and make a stitch horizontally to the left, thus securing the sequin in place **(B)**.

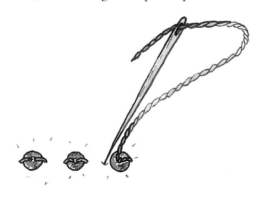

B Secure the sequin with two horizontal stitches.

Attaching sequins using a small bead

Bring the needle up to the front of the fabric and through the holes in the sequin and the bead. Take the needle back down through just the sequin and the fabric **(C)**.

C Anchor the sequin to the fabric with a small bead.

Attaching a line of beads

Bring the beading needle up to the front of the fabric and pick up a few beads on the tip of the needle. Pass the beads along the thread until they are sitting close to the surface of the fabric. Take the needle back down through the fabric, close to the edge of the last bead. Bring the needle up to the surface again, alongside the thread holding the first and second beads. Make a tiny stitch across this thread **(D)**. Continue to make these couching stitches between the beads to secure the whole line. Bring the needle up again beside the last bead and repeat to add more beads.

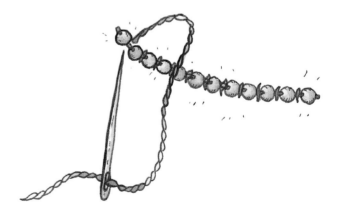

D Secure the thread of beads with tiny couching stitches.

STITCHING

You need just a few basic stitches to complete all the projects in this book. The instructions given for them are for right-handed stitchers; left-handed stitchers may wish to reverse the directions for ease of working.

Starting and finishing a stitch

To start any stitch, knot the end of the thread or work a few unobtrusively placed back stitches on top of each other. Finish off by working a couple of back stitches in the same way.

Slipstitch

Although slipstitch is not a strong stitch, it's very useful where an invisible join between two pieces of folded fabric is required. It produces a neat result with no stitching visible on the surface of the fabric.

After securing the thread, bring the needle up to the surface of the fabric along the folded edge. Insert the needle into the fold on the other piece of fabric, directly opposite, and slide it along the inside of the fold for approximately 0.75cm (¼in). Continue, working from right to left and pulling up the stitches so the folds meet **(A)**.

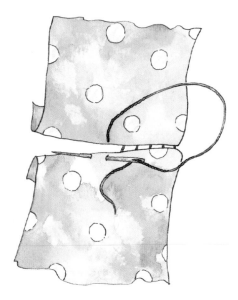

A Gently pull up the slipstitch so it is invisible.

Running, basting, and gathering stitch

Running stitch is worked in different lengths for different purposes. Use a long stitch for basting and gathering, or a shorter one for hand-quilting. Running stitch can also be used as a quick and decorative embroidery stitch.

Secure the thread and then bring the needle up to the surface of the fabric. Working from right to left, pass the needle in and out of the fabric along the stitch line, making stitches of equal length on both sides **(B)**.

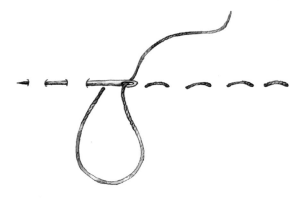

B Make running stitches of equal length.

Stem stitch

Mark out the stitch line with a water-soluble pen. Secure the thread and, working from left to right, bring the needle up to the front of the fabric on the stitch line. Insert the needle a short distance along the line to make the first straight stitch. Bring the needle up again, halfway along and next to the first stitch **(C)**. Take the needle back down through the stitch line to make the next stitch of equal length to the first one. Continue in this way along the stitch line.

C Work stem stitches that evenly overlap.

Blanket stitch

This stitch traditionally is used to edge blankets. Bring the needle up to the front of the fabric at point 1. Insert the needle back down through the fabric at point 2, bringing the tip out at point 3. Loop the thread under the tip of the needle and then pull the thread through **(D)**. Do not pull the thread so tight as to distort the stitch. Repeat to work a row of blanket stitch (*see* Circular Felt Bag, p.26).

Satin stitch

This attractive filling stitch produces a smooth, satin-like finish (*see* Beaded Floral Bag, p.110). Bring the needle up to the front of the fabric at point 1. Reinsert the needle at point 2 and bring it up through the fabric again at point 3. Continue filling in the shape this way, taking great care to keep the tension even and the stitches close and parallel to each other in order to achieve the desired effect **(E)**.

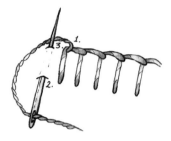

D Loop the thread under the needle to form a blanket stitch.

E Keep stitches close and parallel to create a smooth finish.

Templates

A few of these templates are given at the correct size to make the pattern pieces, but most must be enlarged to the size given on the template before transferring them to the fabric – perhaps done most easily at a copy shop. (The maximum on most copiers is 400 percent.) Follow the instructions on pages 117–18 for transferring the pattern pieces to fabric.

POLO NECK SWEATER BAG
(pp6–11)

Actual width 35cm (14in)
Enlarge to 500% (photocopy at 400%, then 125%)
CUT 2 from face fabric

POLO NECK SWEATER BAG (pp6–11)

Actual length 83cm (32¾in)

Enlarge to 664% (photocopy at 400%, then 166%)
CUT 2 from face fabric

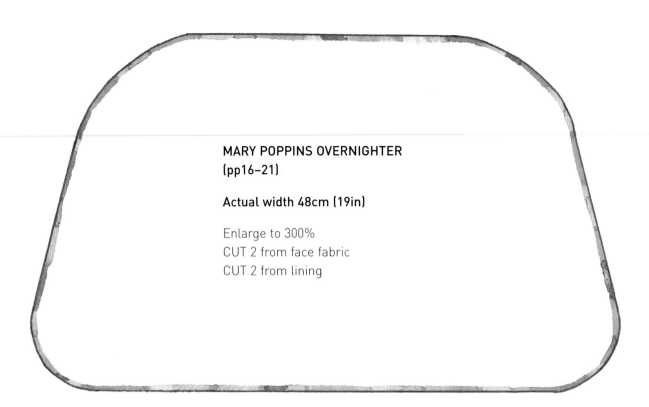

**MARY POPPINS OVERNIGHTER
(pp16–21)**

Actual width 48cm (19in)

Enlarge to 300%
CUT 2 from face fabric
CUT 2 from lining

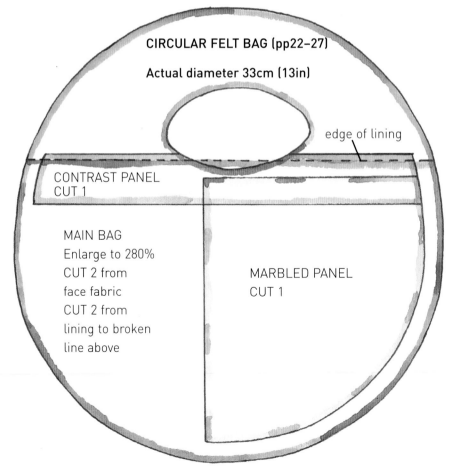

CIRCULAR FELT BAG (pp22–27)

Actual diameter 33cm (13in)

edge of lining

CONTRAST PANEL
CUT 1

MAIN BAG
Enlarge to 280%
CUT 2 from
face fabric
CUT 2 from
lining to broken
line above

MARBLED PANEL
CUT 1

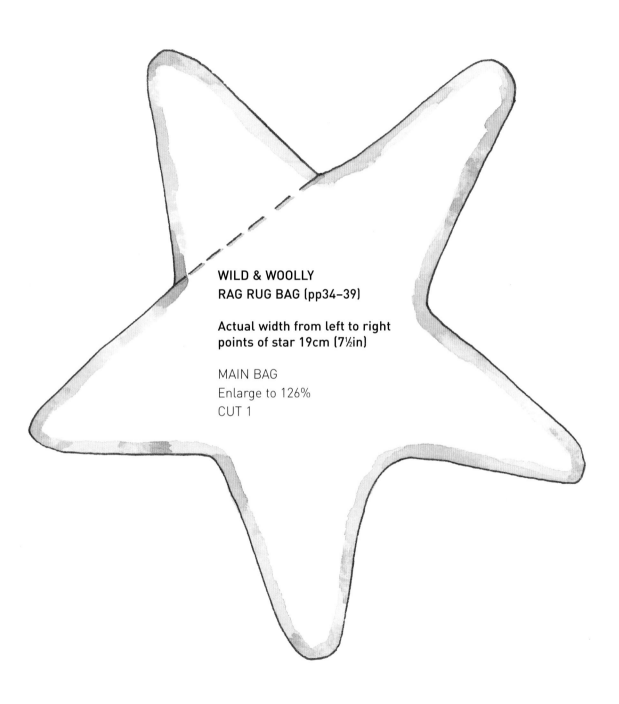

**WILD & WOOLLY
RAG RUG BAG (pp34–39)**

**Actual width from left to right
points of star 19cm (7½in)**

MAIN BAG
Enlarge to 126%
CUT 1

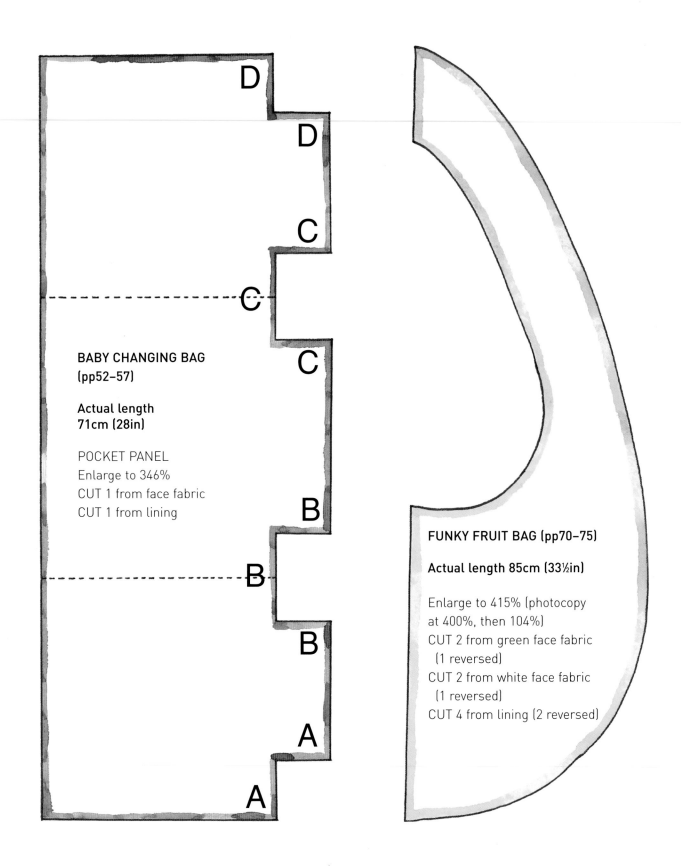

D

D

C

C

BABY CHANGING BAG
(pp52–57)

Actual length
71cm (28in)

POCKET PANEL
Enlarge to 346%
CUT 1 from face fabric
CUT 1 from lining

C

B

B

B

A

A

FUNKY FRUIT BAG (pp70–75)

Actual length 85cm (33½in)

Enlarge to 415% (photocopy
at 400%, then 104%)
CUT 2 from green face fabric
 (1 reversed)
CUT 2 from white face fabric
 (1 reversed)
CUT 4 from lining (2 reversed)

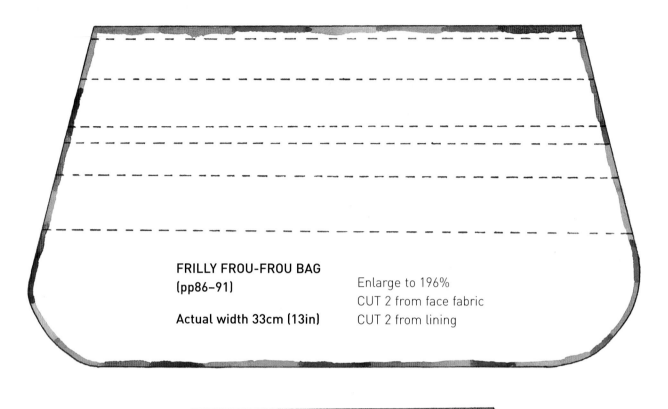

FRILLY FROU-FROU BAG
(pp86–91)

Actual width 33cm (13in)

Enlarge to 196%
CUT 2 from face fabric
CUT 2 from lining

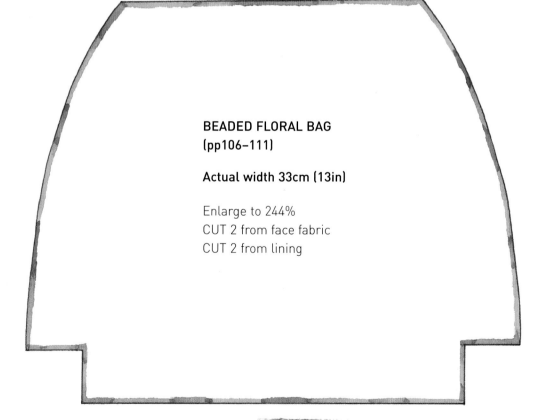

BEADED FLORAL BAG
(pp106–111)

Actual width 33cm (13in)

Enlarge to 244%
CUT 2 from face fabric
CUT 2 from lining

Glossary

Basting (tacking) Sewing to fix temporarily with a loose, long stitch in a soft, easy-to-remove cotton thread. Remove the basting stitches after the main stitching has been done.

Beading needle A very fine long, flexible needle with a sharp point. The fineness enables the needle to pass through even small beads, while the flexibility makes it easy to pick up several small beads at a time, rather than individually.

Bias A line that slants diagonally across a piece of fabric, exactly 45 degrees to the warp and weft.

Binding A strip of fabric used to protect and cover a raw edge. Binding can be purchased, or made from offcuts of fabric. Cut on the bias if the binding needs to wrap smoothly around a curve.

Brooch finding Findings are the metal backings and fixings on decorative items such as brooches and rings. Various types of brooch finding are available. Stitch a ponytail elastic onto a brooch finding to give a corsage even more versatility.

Buckram Extremely firm, almost board-like, gummed cloth used traditionally for stiffening and interlining items such as pelmets and valances. Pelmet stiffener is a modern alternative.

Calico A coarse, inexpensive cotton cloth with a plain weave. Used to make *toiles* (sample pieces), but also as a lining or where a natural, homespun look is required. Available in various qualities and weights, from light, bleached, and very floppy to quite sturdy, unbleached, and with nobbly seeds visible. Choose according to how you want a finished project to look – for example, a stiff calico is pleasantly crisp to the touch and simple to mark, cut, and stitch accurately.

Curved needles Available in a variety of sizes. A medium-fine curved needle will be suitable for all the projects in this book where a curved needle is specified. They are commonly used in upholstery, but are invaluable for stitching easily around tight inner curves and otherwise inaccessible areas.

D-ring A D-shaped metal ring used for joining straps to bags or clothing, often used where a chunky, utilitarian look is required. Available in many sizes and finishes, such as chrome, and also antiqued or shiny brass. Choose a size and finish appropriate to your bag. Sometimes playing with scale can give a lively look, such as using a massive D-ring and very wide strap to funk up an otherwise simple denim tote.

Fusible web This soft webbing contains adhesive, activated by pressing with a hot iron, enabling fabrics to be stuck together without the need for stitching. Available in large sheets, and sold on backing paper, or in strip form for creating hems without stitching. Often referred to by a brand name, rather than this generic term.

Grosgrain ribbon Stiff, durable ribbon woven with a textured ribbed effect; adds a crisp, classic feel to a project.

Gusset A piece of fabric sewn between two seams to give additional width or strength.

Iron-on interfacing Webbing with one side impregnated with adhesive that may be activated by pressing with a hot iron, enabling fabrics to be strengthened, stiffened, and stabilized without the need for an interlining to be stitched in place. Available in various weights. Hold the interlining under your face fabric before purchase and choose according to the desired finished effect. The weight of interlining you choose will dramatically affect the final look of your bag, from boho floppy, using soft interlining, to preppily pristine with firm interlining.

Organza Very fine, quite stiff, transparent, plain woven fabric used decoratively for trims, evening, wedding, and party wear. Available in plain or iridescent shot colours.

Plastic canvas Semi-rigid canvas, made of plastic and with square holes, usually used for needlepoint and cross-stitch items. Also useful in bag-making as a lightweight yet strong stabilizer for the bases and sides of bags that require a crisp, geometric look.

PVA craft adhesive Polyvinyl acetate adhesive: the generic term for a water-based adhesive that is white when applied but dries clear. Available in varying thicknesses: the thicker version, sold as "tacky glue" in craft departments, is especially useful for difficult applications, such as sticking rhinestones to slippery vertical surfaces, where instant grab with a degree of manoeuvrability is required.

Rick-rack braid Flat braid woven into a gently curving zig-zag shape; available in various widths, colours, and fibres.

Tapestry needle A thick, strong needle with a blunt, robust point. Used for needlepoint on canvas, but also where stitching or threading without piercing the fabric is required.

Topstitch A seam on the top face of the work in which the stitches are visible and decorative. Topstitch is worked in either a toning or a contrasting colour.

Wadding/batting Fibrous filling used as an interlining to conserve heat in items such as quilts, ski jackets, and tea cosies, or to achieve a slightly 3-D, puffy effect. Polyester, cotton, wool, and silk waddings are available in varying weights. Choose according to the end use and visual effect required, e.g. a thick polyester wadding makes a comfy baby change mat that is easy to wash and dry quickly, whereas a thin woollen wadding makes a warm, authentic-looking folk-art quilt style for a project that needs less frequent laundering.

Water-soluble fabric marker pen A pen used to apply pattern markings to fabric. The ink can be sponged off gently with cool water.

Index

Acknowledgments

The author would like to thank all those who have helped this project come to fruition. The following have kindly supplied tools and materials:

Silk for beading on the Beaded Floral Bag (pp106–111) from a mouthwatering array of hand-wound silks in varying thicknesses at Mulberry Silks
www.mulberrysilks-patriciawood.com

Handknitted corsage from a wide range of handstitched and knitted flowers, fruit, and foliage at Wild Flower Lanes
www.wildflowerlanes.co.uk

Rag rug yarns from an exciting range of yarns, such as rag, sparkle, recycled paper, and "fuzzi felt", from Rowan Yarns
www.knitrowan.com and www.knitr2.com

Jetstream Elite iron, used throughout for pressing, from Morphy Richards
www.morphyrichards.co.uk

Janome MC9000 sewing machine, used throughout, from Janome
www.janome.co.uk

Non-stick scissors, embroidery scissors, pinking shears, fabric shears, eyelet punches, shape cutters, straight and ripple-edged rotary cutters, used throughout, from an extensive range at Fiskars
www.fiskars.com

Fabric for Mary Poppins Overnighter (pp16–21) from Osborne and Little
www.osborneandlittle.com

Bag for Urban Scrapbook Bag (pp96–99) from a great range of unisex accessories, suitable for customizing, at Fat Face
www.fatface.com

Eyelet kit for Urban Scrapbook Bag (pp96–99) from a wide range of crafts materials at Lakeland Limited
www.lakelandlimited.co.uk

All bags and mood boards designed and illustrated by Deena Beverley
www.deenabeverley.co.uk

Some people have supplied support in more esoteric but no less solidly supporting ways. My heartfelt thanks are due to the friends and family who have sustained me throughout the production of this book in ways too numerous to mention, whether by supplying endless cups of tea and uplifting emails, phone calls, and visits, ferrying my daughter to and from her many activities while I was glued to either the sewing machine or watercolour pad, or by generously sharing their knowledge of all things textile. This category of endlessly patient and generous people includes my husband Andrew and daughter Daisy, M & M, Pat and Chris Cutforth, the Warren family, Holly W, Philip Hudson, Martin Young, Valerie Buck, Jennifer Thompson, Janet Hand, Kathleen Danswan, and all my co-stitchers in the eternally inspiring Embroiderers' Guild. Special thanks are due to my family in Norfolk, who waited patiently for me to emerge from the production of this book at a time when waiting was the hardest thing in the world to do. My grateful thanks in that respect go to my father Keith, Gillian, my sister Nadine and her family, my grandmother Nan Rene, Allan, Josephine and her family. Thanks too of course to Anna Sanderson, Auberon Hedgecoe, Emily Anderson, and Christine Keilty at Mitchell Beazley for bringing my ideas out of my sketchbook and to a wider audience with such commitment, professionalism, trust, and sensitivity.

The author and publisher would like to thank Barbara Mellor and Sue Farr for their proofreading and indexing respectively.

Mitchell Beazley would like to acknowledge and thank the photographers. All photographs are by Roger Dixon except for those on the following pages, which are by Andrew Newton-Cox: 3, 5, 103, 106, 107, 109, 112, 113, 115.